"If you feel disillusioned in your [...] you to new commitment. If you [...] cracked up to be, this book will challenge you to serve your spouse unselfishly. If you wonder what the Bible has to say about marriage, this book will enlighten your spiritual eyes. Or if you just want to deepen your great love, this book will give you a shot of encouragement. Every couple should read this book!"

KATHY COLLARD MILLER AND LARRY MILLER
Authors of *When the Honeymoon's Over* and
What's in the Bible for Couples

"I've often said that anyone who thinks their marriage is going to be perfect is probably still at their reception! Marriage requires work, understanding, patience, love, faith, forgiveness, and a healthy sense of humor. In *One True Vow*, gifted writer and speaker Eva Marie Everson reminds readers of the power of the marriage vow. More than simple words spoken ten, twenty, even fifty years ago, the marriage vow is a safety net capable of holding up under the weight of whatever life throws our way. So, no matter how many years you've been married, or even if you're just engaged, read this book and be encouraged. Your marriage deserves it!"

MARTHA BOLTON
Comedy Writer and
Author of *I Love You. . .Still: To Keep Love You Gotta Laugh*

"*One True Vow* picks up where most romance novels leave off. They end with the wedding because the day-to-day stuff of making a marriage work isn't nearly as romantic—often it is rough! *One True Vow* restores our faith in not just the romance of the relationship but the reality of keeping that vow and making the marriage work. It is inspiring and instructional as you learn from the true lives of others."

MARITA LITTAUER AND CHUCK NOON
Authors of *Love Extravagantly*

"*One True Vow* shows how to work through whatever life brings so that your marriage works for life. Very helpful and very real. I loved it!"

LINDA EVANS SHEPHERD,
President,
Right to the Heart Ministries

"My heart loves a good story! In this inspiring and sobering group of stories, Eva Marie uses the rich details of real-life relationships as a window into life after the tuxedos are returned and the honeymoon is over. Prepare to blush—the raw honesty of these stories lead us to levels of truth and power that every couple needs in order to keep their one true vow!"

KEVIN URICHKO
Pastor of Small Groups
Northland, A Church Distributed

One True Vow

*Love Stories of
Faith and Commitment*

EVA MARIE EVERSON

PROMISE
PRESS
An Imprint of Barbour Publishing

Member of the
Evangelical Christian
Publishers Association

Printed in the United States of America.

Dedicated to . . .

Joel and Becky Hunter
Thank you for your endless
examples of true love and commitment. . .and
for allowing me to use so many of
your fine examples of teaching.

And to my brother. . .

$\mathcal{J}$ guarantee that we'll have tough times,
and I guarantee that at some point
one or both of us will want to get out.
But I also guarantee that if I don't ask you to be mine,
I'll regret it for the rest of my life.
Because I know in my heart, you're the only one for me.

RICHARD GERE AND JULIA ROBERTS
Runaway Bride
Paramount Pictures & Touchstone Pictures 1999

Acknowledgments

*W*hile working on my first book for Promise Press *(True Love: Engaging Stories of Real-Life Proposals)*, I spent countless hours reading the marriage proposals of over fifty couples. They were all precious stories, but what captivated me most were the addendums, such as, "We've been married for over fifty years." "We experienced many setbacks, lost one of our children to death." "My husband recently had a heart attack." "Still, we love each other very much and I wouldn't trade a minute of our lives together."

> *Wow!* I thought. *Now, these are the stories!* So I immediately went to my editor, Susan Schlabach, and relayed that thought. Susan agreed, asked to see a proposal for the book, and the next thing I knew *this* book was in progress. So let me begin by thanking Susan and Promise Press for the opportunity, once again, to tell the stories of truly inspirational people. ("Susan, writing these stories is *really hard!*" "Just stay with it, Eva.") I'd also like to thank my agent, Mr. William Watkins, for his words of wisdom and for his belief in me, and the talent God gave me. ("Bill, do you have a minute to talk?") A special "thanks" goes to Karen Berry Johnson for helping with copyright issues. ("Karen, you're the only one I know who might know someone who knows someone!")
>
> Again, "Thank you!" to CLASServices, Inc. and staff. You are such a blessing!

A huge thank-you goes to my husband and children, who allowed me to "hole up" in my home office for hours on end. ("Jessica, *please* turn your music down. . . Dennis, can you fix dinner tonight. . .oh, and maybe actually go grocery shopping, too. . . Ashley, move over, child. . . Sarah, stop talking; I have a deadline. Jordynn, isn't it time for your nap?")

Thank you, all of you, who sent your stories and allowed me into some of the most difficult days, months, and years of your lives.

Most of all, of course, thank You, heavenly Father, from whom all blessings flow. ("It's me again, Father. I'm not so sure I can do this. . . .") Through Him all things are possible. Amen.

Foreword

*"For better, for worse, for richer, for poorer,
in sickness and in health. . ."*

I cry at weddings these days. For years I sat in the hard oak pews of churches and smiled broadly. As I watched the ceremony, I pictured Cinderella and her Prince Charming riding away in a golden carriage to his castle perched high atop happily-ever-after. But I've been married for over twenty-two years, and I know that fairy tales are for children's bookshelves. So now I cry at weddings. I cry because I understand the commitment and I know that while the bride and groom *think* they perceive the true depth of their vows, they don't. They *say,* "For better, for worse, for richer, for poorer, in sickness and in health," but what they *hear* is, "For *better,* for *richer,* and *in health.*" Surely, they surmise, nothing could go wrong in our marriage. . .not when two people are so very much in love as we are!

Ask anyone who's been married any length of time and they'll tell you, the tests of the vow *will* come, and as love is tried, God remains faithful to those who put their trust in Him.

What can test a marriage vow? Anything! Yes, the obvious things. . .things like infidelity, addictions, loss of income or property, and chronic illnesses or death. But there are other things. . .innocent in appearance. . .which can chink away at the armor of marriage until there is nothing left but shredded tin. Things like checkbooks and credit cards, theology, blended families, the birth of a child, job promotions, remodeling a home, an empty nest, or expectation misunderstandings. . .like, who gets to take out the garbage and whose turn it is to walk the dog.

Aren't some of those the things that can bring couples closer to one another? Ideally, with compromise, yes. Typically. . .no.

I learned a lot from my grandmother about the sacredness of wedding vows. She stood in the middle of the Georgia pines and spoke her vows before the justice of the peace and his wife. First and foremost, though, she spoke her vows before God, and she honored that commitment in spite of the years of tumult that followed. In the early years, she told me, my grandfather made certain that there was food on the table, but the rest of his paycheck he "drank." As we sat at her kitchen table, sipping coffee and eating cake, she confided that it was no secret to her that he had "an eye for a skirt." But, she stated emphatically, "he never hit me." I shake my head in wonder at this kind of devotion. "Grandmama," I asked her, "why did you stay?"

Her answer can be found within the pages of this book, and not just within her words, but within the words of those who have been faithful to their marriage vows.

On my twenty-first wedding anniversary, my husband received a phone call from an old friend. I was exercising my spousal rights of eavesdropping when I heard my husband say, "Yep! Twenty-one years today. . .thank you. . . ." Then there was a long pause. The man on the other end of the line must have commented on how remarkable it is to hear of a man and woman loving each other for twenty-one years, because my husband's next comment was, "It's not about loving each other for twenty-one years. It's not about loving each other every day for the rest of your lives, or even liking each other. In fact, there are times when you don't like each other at all! But what it is about is a commitment. . .a commitment that says, 'No matter what. . .come what may. . .I'll be here for you forever.'"

I agree. We may not like the circumstances we are living in; we may want to jump ship and run, but those are not the vows we took. We took vows that said forever and that's just the way it's going to be! That's what it's about, really. It's about staying true to the vow, trusting God, and knowing that beyond each low valley there's a high mountain and beyond each difficult-to-climb mountain, there's a peaceful valley.

My husband presented me with a beautiful pair of earrings for our twenty-first anniversary. He truly believes that was his gift to me. Truth is, the best gift was the words of commitment he spoke to his friend, overheard by my loving heart.

The stories in this book are as varied as the people who lived them, but all of them are true and represent a time when the contributors felt their vows were being tested. Some will make you laugh and others will make you cry. You will identify with several, and thank God you've never lived through the rest. In the end, you will see that nothing is impossible with God and that by Him all things are held together (Mark 10:27 and Colossians 1:17, author's paraphrase).

My prayer for each of you, especially if you are experiencing a rough place in the road, is that you will find hope, help, and encouragement within these pages. . .and that you will know how very much God loves you and wants only good things for you.

EVA MARIE EVERSON

When you commit to something for the first time, you think you're committing to one thing and you're really committing to something you haven't experienced yet. So, you don't have a clue. Now that doesn't mean you don't commit. When you got married, you thought you knew what you were committing to. You didn't have a clue. You just didn't know.

DR. JOEL HUNTER

Be strong and courageous.
Do not be terrified; do not be discouraged,
for the LORD your God will be with you wherever you go."

JOSHUA 1:9

A Marriage

You are holding up a ceiling
with both arms. It is very heavy,
but you must hold it up, or else
it will fall down on you. Your arms
are tired, terribly tired,
and, as the day goes on, it feels
as if either your arms or the ceiling
will soon collapse.
But then,
unexpectedly,
something wonderful happens:
someone:
a man or a woman,
walks into the room
and holds their arms up
to the ceiling beside you.

So you finally get
to take down your arms.
You feel the relief of respite,
the blood flowing back
to your fingers and arms.
And when your partner's arms tire,
you hold up your own
to relieve him again.

And it can go on like this
for many years
without the house falling.

MICHAEL BLUMENTHAL

J can sing in front of fifty thousand people and not be afraid at all. But singing at weddings scares me to death. The biggest day of my friends' lives, videotapes rolling, parents in the wings, and I could single-handedly mess it up with a song I don't know. So I thought the best thing I could do was write my own song for just such a day. I drew my inspiration from the great love in my life, and I believe that a love between a man and woman is one of the greatest symbols for the spiritual love of our Creator. I know that it has been in my life.[1]

GEOFF MOORE†
(Speaking of his song,
"If You Could See What I See,"
written with Steven Curtis Chapman)

FOR BETTER. . .
FOR WORSE. . .

In the marriage ceremony, that moment when falling in love
   is replaced by the arduous drama of staying in love,
   the words "in sickness and in health, for richer, for poorer,
   till death do us part" set love in the temporal context in
   which it achieves its meaning.

    As time begins to elapse, one begins to love the other
because they have shared the same experience. . .
Selves may not intertwine; but lives do,
and shared memory becomes as much of a bond
as the bond of the flesh. . .

MICHAEL IGNATIEFF,
from *Lodged in the Heart and Memory*

I want to give you a very important principle for the answering of the world's problems. Here's the principle: We do not win by power, or rank, or authority. We only win by intimacy. We do not win by calculating how we can overcome the opposition. We only win by getting closer to people and getting closer to God.

DR. JOEL HUNTER

I liked my marriage as long as Alvin was nice to me.
It was a bargain—he was good to me,
so I was good to him.
That's not what marriage is about at all.

CECE WINANS

Dick and I promised each other that "if we hadn't felt heard, we would stop the other, sit them down, and say it again." This wasn't always easy, but we did it. This kept our hurts little when spoken. It also kept anger from enlarging a problem.

PAULA S. MITCHELL,
Married May 19, 1984;
temporarily separated by death September 20, 1999

Anyone can be passionate,
but it takes real lovers to be silly.

ROSE FRANKEN

It was a rare occurrence; my wife and I were alone and in control of the living room for an entire evening. Typically, our son and a few of his friends take up the couch and television as we go to other, more quiet, places in the house. Should there happen to be a basketball game that I want to watch, I'll watch it on the small television in the kitchen. My wife, Kim, rarely joins me since we don't share the same interests in each other's programs. Plus, there's the problem of the remote control. Whoever has possession of the "channel-changer" can't resist seeing what's being missed on the other channels. The person "not in charge" tends to become aggravated.

But on this evening we sat together on the couch for awhile before we turned on the television to see what might be on. My wife handed the remote to me. I flipped around to a couple of programs and finally settled on a CBS special. I didn't find it particularly interesting, but my wife seemed to enjoy it. We sat there together, watching the program and talking during the commercials. It was turning into a very nice, romantic time together. Eventually I made some comment about the program that caused my wife to ask me if I was interested in what we had been watching. "No," I answered honestly. "I left the remote alone because I thought you were watching the program."

Then she said the funniest thing. "I don't find the program all that great! I was watching it because I thought you were enjoying it!" We looked at each other for a moment and then we started to laugh. The remote control can actually bring us closer to each other. . .especially when we leave it alone.

PAUL BUDD

Paul and Kim's Precious Verse:

"The thief comes only to steal and kill and destroy; I have come that they may have life, and have it to the full."

JOHN 10:10

Love one another and you will be happy. It's as simple and as difficult as that.

MICHAEL LEUNIG

God's Battle

Tom and Elizabeth Harper*

*L*et me ask you this: Have the decisions you've made in the last six months pleased the Lord?"

---

*Here and throughout book, indicates the names have been changed at the subjects' request.

The guest speaker at Elizabeth Harper's church in West-over, Pennsylvania, struck a nerve one Sunday morning and it vibrated deep within her heart. *Have they?* she asked herself while sitting in the pew. Again, that afternoon, as she sat in the quietness of her home and forced herself to think about the events of the past year, the question arose. *Have they?*

A year ago, Elizabeth would not have guessed this question would grip her heart in such a vise. One winter's evening, as she and her husband, Tom, sat snuggled together in their Pennsylvania-mountains home, a strange thought came to her mind. "Do you ever wonder what it would be like to be alone?" she asked.

"It scares me," Tom replied. The fire in the fireplace crack-led nearby, shedding light on his dark, handsome face. "I don't even like to think about it."

Elizabeth smiled and snuggled closer to her husband. Yes, she had it all, she thought. A marriage on rock-solid ground, a job she enjoyed, a beautiful home, and a loving, godly husband. She closed her eyes and allowed herself to bask in the moment.

On Christmas Sunday, Tom and Elizabeth attended a special service at another church where they met Annie and Jack. Annie, always full of theological questions, warmed instantly to Tom, ever the wise Bible student. Over the next number of weeks, as the two couples began to meet for dinner or evenings spent in each other's homes, Annie and Tom kept the conversation lively.

Yet, in spite of the comfortable banter, Elizabeth was begin-ning to feel uneasy. Annie's eyes twinkled when she laughed at Tom's jokes, in strong contrast to Jack's quiet soberness.

"Annie is so interesting," Tom observed. "She came by the shop today and we had another Bible debate," he added. As the days pressed forward, Elizabeth continued to hear Tom's praises of Annie. "Annie is so funny." "Annie is so cute."

"Come on, Tom!" Elizabeth finally confronted her husband, though she kept her eyes on the laundry she had been folding. "Aren't you getting a little overly involved in these discussions?"

Tom drew back as though a snake had bitten him. "I'm just helping her to understand the Bible better," he replied coolly.

The frequent reports and comments about Annie ended, but as months went by, a chill Elizabeth and Tom had never before experienced began to permeate their home. With the exception of Elizabeth's attempts to discuss the issue, conversation was nearly nonexistent.

"Can't you see this is hurting our relationship?" she asked.

"You're the one having the trouble. Annie has nothing to do with it."

Other attempts followed. "Tom, why don't we plan a trip together soon?"

"Why? We aren't interested in the same things."

*We used to be. . .*Elizabeth thought sadly.

Eventually, the emotional distance was joined by a physical one, and Tom began to spend longer hours at work.

One night Elizabeth exploded. "Can't we settle this?"

"What's there to settle? You get upset over nothing."

The home that had once been a loving haven for Elizabeth and Tom was now a place of escalating tension, stress, and anxiety. One afternoon in June, Tom stomped into the house and headed straight for the shower.

"Where are you going?" Elizabeth asked.

"I'm going to a Bible study with Annie and Jack," he answered. "And if you say anything about it, I'm leaving at the end of the month."

Elizabeth's pent-up anger rose to the surface and burst furiously out of her. "The end of the month? If you aren't willing to be a husband here, then make it now!"

Tom brushed past Elizabeth and began to gather his clothes from the bureau drawers and closets. He didn't even bother to throw them in a suitcase; he held as much as he could carry in his arms and stormed out, slamming the door behind him.

Elizabeth sat in the silence that echoed the shouting, staring at the closed door. "Surely he will return any minute," she told herself. By evening, however, she instinctively knew Tom would not be coming home. Months of struggling and the intense pressure to bridge the gap that had formed between them was over. As the silence enveloped her, Elizabeth realized that what once had been her enemy was now her friend. The house wasn't *silent;* it was *quiet.*

That night Elizabeth slept well and woke the next morning with renewed energy. *This house is peaceful,* she thought. As she swung her legs off the side of the bed, she became aware of a lightheartedness she hadn't felt in months. Though mentally it didn't seem right, it was as if a heavy weight had been lifted from her shoulders.

Maybe he'll stay away, Elizabeth caught herself thinking. *If he wants to return, I'll dissuade him. "No," I'll say. "We're better off this way."*

Elizabeth never got to say the rehearsed words. That day, while she was at work, Tom returned for the remainder of his possessions.

Just as well, she thought. *It might have turned ugly.*

It all seemed so easy. Even confronting friends and family wasn't as difficult as Elizabeth had expected. Some time later, when she was laid off from her job and had to scrimp to pay bills, Elizabeth continued to weather the storm with a quiet calm.

"Tom is staying with Annie and Jack," friends told her. Other friends felt it necessary to report Tom's activities. "I saw

Tom the other day," she would hear.

Elizabeth felt a twist of irony. She didn't care where Tom was staying or what he was doing. She only wanted to bask in her newfound peace. . .that is, until the morning the visiting pastor stood behind the pulpit and said, "Have the decisions you've made in the last six months pleased the Lord?"

The following week was spent with that haunting question. Elizabeth knew the answer was "no." Even though separation felt best, she had to ask herself, *Is it?*

Early Saturday morning, on his way to a festival, Tom stopped by the house to pick up some papers. Elizabeth's guard was down, and when he strolled in looking cheerful, handsome, and sporty, she was stunned.

"I need these notarized," he offered, indicating the papers in his hand.

Elizabeth nodded, and when he walked out, she dissolved into tears. Slipping down to her knees, she called out to God. "Oh, Lord, forgive me! I have sinned against Tom and I have sinned against You with my bitterness. I want to resolve our marriage. Oh, Lord, I remember the story of the prodigal son and right now I feel just as he must have. My life is in a downward spiral. I'm empty. Wasted. Without purpose. But like the son, I remember that my Father's hired servants have bread to spare while I perish from hunger. Like the son, I know that I should return to the vows I spoke to Tom before You. I should try again." Elizabeth took a deep breath before adding, "But Tom will have to change, too. I'll give it until the end of the year. If things are no different then, I'll take it as a sign there will be no going back."

For two days, Elizabeth was confident her prayer would be answered, but on Monday doubt surfaced. *Tom is a guest in someone else's home. . .he has freedom. . .no responsibilities. He talks differently. He dresses differently. I'm not sure I know him anymore. How, then, can I ever approach him?*

A few days later, the washing machine broke down and Elizabeth called Tom, asking for help.

"I can come Thursday evening to look at it," he told her.

"Would you like to come for dinner?" Elizabeth's voice reflected a new shyness between the two of them.

A long moment of silence followed before Tom agreed. "Yeah. Sure."

For the next three days, Elizabeth was as nervous as a teenager waiting for her first date. "Lord God," she prayed, "will this man I've spent intimate time with return as the stranger who left? Or will he, too, want to restore our relationship? Will You change him, as I've prayed that You will? Because, if not, things will surely never work out."

Thursday evening, after the machine was repaired and dinner had been eaten, Elizabeth and Tom had engaged in awkward conversation while sitting apart on the sofa. When he left, Elizabeth walked Tom to the door. As he looked down at her, she reached up to kiss him but was stopped by his biting words.

"Look," he said, "I'm not coming back. It took me a long time to get over the pain. I don't want to hurt like that again."

"I don't either," Elizabeth whispered, then watched as Tom slipped out the opened door. Pressing her head against it after it closed, she began to cry. "It's hopeless," she sobbed.

Later that evening, Elizabeth sat with her open Bible across her lap as she searched its pages for what comfort she might be able to find.

"The LORD says to you: '. . .the battle is not yours, but God's' " (2 Chronicles 20:15).

Elizabeth read the words not once but again and again. *How clear this is,* she thought. "Lord, if the battle is not mine, then it's not for me to decide whether or not Tom should change. Heaven knows I can scarcely change myself! I will trust You and wait to see what You will do."

The following week, Elizabeth called Tom again. "Would you like to take me to dinner?" she asked, bolder than she had been the week before.

Tom was surprised and amused. "I can do that," he said.

Their dinner date was much more comfortable than it had been the week before. They talked freely, and at the end of the evening, Tom kissed Elizabeth for the first time since he had walked out the door.

An excited Elizabeth reported the changes to her pastor.

"Don't move too quickly or be deceived by little encouragements," he said.

His counsel was right on the money. At times the rebuilding of Elizabeth and Tom's relationship was rocky and uncertain. Some days things seemed to be moving toward a healing, but the very next day, Tom would interpret a comment of Elizabeth's as critical, and he would blow up and then retreat.

"Lord, there's still so much that needs to be changed!" she prayed fervently. Yet, to her amazement, it was Elizabeth who was changing, becoming softer and more flexible.

Weeks turned to months. Autumn's beautiful foliage turned to bleak grays and browns. Still, Elizabeth continued to pray for the resolution that didn't seem to be happening. "It's been a long time, Lord," she said. "I'm no longer living in the future. Tom and I have had these moments and I treasure them. If there's no reunion, at least I have a new, accepting attitude with which to live my solitary life."

In late December, six months after leaving, Tom came to the house. When Elizabeth greeted him, he walked to the sofa and sat on its edge, staring solemnly at the floor.

Elizabeth sat beside him. "Tom, what's wrong?"

"I can't live like this anymore," he said quietly. "I don't know if coming back is right or not, but I'm willing to give it a try."

With that, he moved back home.

"Happily Ever After" didn't happen right away; there were nights when Tom chose to sleep in the guest room or remain at work.

"The battle is not yours, it's Mine," the Lord would remind Elizabeth. "You have to accept Tom as he is. . .and not only Tom. There is no one you can change, really. You must learn to accept all people just as they are."

Ten years have passed. The home that had once been wracked by angry separation is again a haven of peace. Battles arise, but they are God's, not Elizabeth's. He has taught her to love Tom for who he is, not for who she wishes he would be. This is, after all, God's kind of love. This is unconditional love.

Tom and Elizabeth's Precious Verse:

"This is what the LORD says to you: 'Do not be afraid or discouraged because of this vast army. For the battle is not yours, but God's.' "   2 CHRONICLES 20:15

*Chains do not hold a marriage together.
It is threads, hundreds of tiny threads,
which sew people together through the years.*

SIMONE SIGNORET

25

*Marriage should be honored by all,
and the marriage bed kept pure,
for God will judge
the adulterer and
all the sexually immoral.*

HEBREWS 13:4

The Spark Is Back[†]

Herb and Marcia Anderson*

Marcia Anderson stood at the front window and peeked out.

"What are you looking at?" her husband, Herb, said from behind her. The smell of freshly brewed coffee wafted from the coffee mug he held in his hand.

Marcia turned and smiled. "I'm watching Jim getting the paper."

Herb stepped up behind Marcia and peered through the slit in the blinds. "Ten to one Jan is standing at the front door waiting for him," he said with a chuckle as they moved away from the window.

"They certainly are joined at the hip," Marcia said. "Did you know that in twenty years of marriage, they've only been separated three nights?"

[†] Here and throughout book, indicates the couple's story can be found in *True Love: Engaging Stories of Real-Life Proposals* by Eva Marie Everson.

"They're cute, you know. I see them walking through the neighborhood together, buying groceries together, gardening together. Sometimes I wonder how either of them will cope when the other dies. The word *traumatic* may not begin to cover the circumstance."

"Only three days apart! So different from us, huh?"

Indeed. Because of business travel, Marcia and Herb had been separated for half of their first twelve years of marriage. They didn't think about it; it was just a fact of life. Even their dogs adjusted. Like clockwork, when instinct told them the master was due home, they waited patiently by the front window, with their ears perked and tails wagging in unison.

For the most part, Marcia and her pets had adapted well. Unfortunately, whenever something went wrong with the house, her car, or should she become ill, it always seemed to fall within Herb's travel time. One afternoon, as she stepped into the foyer of their home after taking a cab from a service station, she spoke out loud, "Well! Marriage certainly isn't the fairy tale bridal magazines would have one believe!"

Later that night, as she spoke with Herb about the circumstances that had forced her to a service station and then to call a cab, she said, "I feel like I'm existing without the other half of me!"

"I'm sorry, Honey. I really wish I was there to help you, but until I am, I suppose you'll have to handle all these things yourself."

Learn she did! "Did you know," she told Herb across the miles one evening, "that if the chain in the toilet breaks in the middle of the night, paper clips are a handy substitute?"

Herb laughed. "No, I didn't know that!"

"Did you know that when the vacuum cleaner breaks down and it's too heavy to get into the trunk of my car, a damp sponge mop will pick up a great deal of lint?"

"It appears that my wife has learned to be creative!"

At the end of the first twelve years of their marriage, Herb came home with news. "I've been promoted," he said. "We're being transferred to a larger city. The really good news is that I won't be traveling every other week from now on."

"Herb, that's fantastic!" Marcia said enthusiastically, totally unaware of the changes she would be forced to make.

It was more than leaving her job as a music teacher; moving from one city to the next involved more than a new house and learning the directions to the nearest supermarket. There were new friendships to be formed, a new church to fit into, and the quest for a new job. The search for the latter fell into place providentially.

One afternoon, Marcia walked into the local newspaper to subscribe. When she walked out, she was the new entertainment reviewer.

"This is certainly a change in profession!" Herb exclaimed.

"I know!" Marcia said. "I will still teach music, but this job will have me reviewing concerts, films, plays. . .that sort of thing."

Over the next few years, Herb got a taste of what Marcia had lived through during his years of absence. She was away from home most evenings while he, tired from work, stayed home with their dogs.

"The dishwasher overflowed," Herb said, meeting Marcia at the door late one evening.

"And?"

"I didn't know what to do!" he complained.

Another evening Marcia heard, "The dog threw up on the carpet while you were gone tonight."

"Did you clean it up?" Marcia asked wearily.

"No," Herb said. "I wasn't sure how. I waited 'til you got home."

"Great," Marcia moaned.

Eventually things came to a head. "I think you and I need to get away from work and the city so we can talk things through," Marcia suggested. "What do you think?"

"I think so, too," Herb agreed.

A few days later, in the midst of their vacation, they faced each other.

"Did you ever *ask* me if I was dissatisfied with your traveling?" Marcia asked.

"No, but did you ever *tell me* you were dissatisfied with it?"

"No. No, I didn't."

"I guess now I know how you felt."

"You've never expressed dissatisfaction with my job, Herb."

"Marcia, you never even asked me what would happen if you took that job. You never indicated that you'd be gone so many nights."

Marcia nodded in understanding. Over the next few days, feelings poured out. When the vacation was over, Marcia and Herb saw each other in a new light and they had a new plan.

The following week, as Marcia scheduled her review of the symphony a few nights later, she picked up the phone and called Herb at work. "Would you like to go to the symphony with me on Thursday?"

"Absolutely. I'm glad you called, too. I was wondering if you would like to go with me to a business luncheon on Tuesday."

Marcia smiled knowingly. "I would love it!"

"It's a date, then. Thursday the symphony and Tuesday the luncheon."

The spark was back. . . .

One morning, as Marcia put the final touches on an article she was writing for the newspaper, the phone rang. It was Herb, calling from his business trip to Nebraska. "The heater in my room isn't working," he reported.

"Herb, wouldn't it make more sense to call the front desk than to call me?"

"Oh. Oh, yeah," he replied with a chuckle.

*Ah, men. . .*Marcia thought with a smile. *You gotta love 'em!*

Herb and Marcia's Precious Verse:

"But blessed is the man who trusts in the LORD, whose confidence is in him. He will be like a tree planted by the water that sends out its roots by the stream. It does not fear when heat comes; its leaves are always green. It has no worries in a year of drought and never fails to bear fruit."

JEREMIAH 17:7–8

We cannot change anything until we accept it. Condemnation does not liberate, it oppresses.

C. G. JUNG

I have to be honest with you; our religious backgrounds are different. When I was eighteen years old, this wasn't the governing factor when we said, "I do." However, I can tell you this, in retrospect, it *does* matter. It really does make a huge difference if you are both on the same plane with respects to your faith, because it's a very intimate part of yourself that you really want to share. With that said, let me continue: It's not easy. It takes a great deal of work—teamwork—for a marriage to last. When one person becomes self-centered, or "self-anything" for that matter, then the team integrity is weakened. Communication is key. Once you stop talking (and listening)...then it's over. Most of us don't have a problem with talking; it's the listening part that challenges us. There are so many elements to making it "work." Love. Respect. Humility. Forgiveness. We've certainly had our trials and tribulations. After Bruce and I had our third child, we lost our first house, filed bankruptcy, and then we had to move in with my parents, who helped us recoup. When that didn't work out, we left and lived on the beach in a tent for a week. Still, we loved... we respected...we showed humility, and we forgave. So to conclude: It's all about hard work. You really have to work hard in all areas in your life to succeed...a marriage is no different.

SHARON LLEWELLYN,
Married July 16, 1984

*O*nly in the agony of parting
do we look into the depths of love.

GEORGE ELIOT

*L*ove is an act of endless forgiveness,
a tender look which becomes a habit.

PETER USTINOV

The Retrouvaille Experience

Galen and Pat Smith

"What am I doing wrong?" Pat Smith cried to her husband of just four years. "I am a good wife and mother. I help earn the income. Just what is it that keeps you so angry all the time?"

As far as Pat could see, her husband, Galen, never saw things her way. Then again, she rarely saw things his way either. For most of their marriage they argued, blamed, accused, and found fault with each other. They separated twice. In spite of Galen's filing for divorce during one of the separations, they spoke each and every night on the telephone. The conversations, however, always ended in another hot flash of temper and accusations.

After six horrible weeks, they reconciled, and things were good. . .for about a week. Then the fighting began again.

"We're just two misery-filled people," Galen said. "That's all I know to say to you."

In January 1990, when Pat thought their marriage could take no more stress and another separation occurred, she called their priest, Fr. Jerry Calhoun.

"We need help, Father. We've tried everything else; maybe it's time to seek spiritual help."

Father Jerry smiled at the irony. "Let me make a suggestion to you, Pat. Retrouvaille is a weekend program for married couples. They use a new technique of communication and presentations focusing on three specific areas of marriage. It will help you put the past behind you and help you rediscover the love you have for each other. Why don't you and Galen look into that?"

Pat relayed the suggestion to Galen and he reluctantly agreed. Pat filled out applications for the marriage retreat, and they were screened by telephone.

"Are both of you committed to trying to make your marriage work?" they were asked.

"Yes," Pat and Galen answered.

"You must be willing to give up 'third-party relationships' if there are any."

"There aren't, thank God," Pat answered.

"If you have any addictions—drugs or alcohol—you must be willing to deal with that first."

"We stopped drinking two years ago," Galen reported. "We knew that consumption of alcohol only escalated our arguments."

"Good. We'll be seeing you soon, then."

The weekend of the retreat finally arrived. Galen picked Pat up at her office after work. Both were nursing colds, and Galen appeared to have added a bad mood to his illness. Pat immediately sensed something evil trying to come between her and her husband. As Galen picked for an argument, she went to the Lord in prayer. *God, if I can just keep quiet and not argue with him for the seventy-mile trip, I know You will give us the help we need.*

During the hour-and-a-half drive, Pat reflected on the various methods to save their marriage they'd tried in the past, including a psychiatrist who said, "I have an eight-week program you can come to for counseling. But I don't really care one way or the other if your marriage works out. I'll just mediate for you and let you decide." That was their first and last session.

Pat and Galen entered into the Retrouvaille process on Friday evening. They were welcomed warmly by the other couples who made the fall retreat. After everyone had settled in, the first session began. Pat squirmed in her seat as she looked over at her husband. *Is he paying attention? Will this help him?*

Pat suddenly stopped in her finger-pointing and began to

listen to the presenter. *This isn't just Galen's problem. I'm in trouble, too.*

Pat turned her pointing finger at herself.

By the end of the retreat, Galen and Pat were aware of three things:

1) God wanted their marriage to survive,
2) the two of them and their little son, Tony, had suffered a terrible loss, and
3) they needed to get back to the way they had felt when they first met, fell in love, and married. This meant a painful look backward, but only long enough to heal.

Pat and Galen cried cleansing tears as they worked quietly with God through their problems. Healing the hurts meant more than saying, "I'm sorry." It also meant, "Please forgive me for what I have done and what I have failed to do."

Over a decade has passed. Pat and Galen have continued to mature in the Lord and within the sacredness of their marriage. Galen has a full-time job, writes part-time, and serves as publisher and editor of *UpSouth,* a newsletter for Catholic and Southern writers. Galen also hosts a television show by the same name. Pat also works full time and is a paid correspondent for *Western Kentucky Catholic.* She writes a monthly column titled "Living the Sacraments: The Catholic Woman's Role" and writes for other periodicals as well.

Yes, they still have disagreements. They still argue, but now they clear the air. They occasionally fuss, cry, and fume; but they don't leave. Pat and Galen know there will always be ups and downs in their marriage; but at the end of the day, they also know they are committed to each other.

Better still, they are in love.

One True Vow

Galen and Pat's Precious Verse:

Trust in the LORD with all your heart and lean not on your own understanding; in all your ways acknowledge him, and he will make your paths straight.   PROVERBS 3:5–6

There is nothing nobler or more admirable
than when two people
who see eye to eye keep house as man and wife,
confounding their enemies and delighting their friends.

HOMER, *The Odyssey*

Unless the LORD builds the house, its builders labor in vain. Unless the LORD watches over the city, the watchmen stand guard in vain.

PSALM 127:1

My husband, Dennis, was the son of a minister and a homemaker, the fourth of six children. In spite of their Christianity, his parents had grown up in an era when it was considered wrong to show emotions toward people in public. . .and public meant in front of their children, too. As a result, Dennis never saw his parents show their feelings, whether good or bad, for one another.

My father worked in a steel foundry and my mother was a shoe factory worker. My father was not a Christian. He'd grown up in a family with a history of alcoholism, depression, and little expressed love. These weaknesses revealed themselves in many abusive ways in our home, causing my brothers and me to suffer greatly at the hands of our father. My mother claimed she was a Christian, but I'm not sure she had a personal relationship with Jesus. If she did, it was never evident to me. As kids we were taken to church pretty regularly, so I had a nodding acquaintance with the Christmas and Easter stories, at least the baby in a manger and palm branch waving portions of those stories. In fifteen years, though, I cannot recall hearing the reason for those stories or how they could personally affect my life.

Dennis and I met in October 1971 when I was fourteen years old. Right away, I knew there was something different about him. He was unlike all the other guys I'd known. Dennis was gentle, kind, loving, and trusting. I was just the opposite. The abuse during my early years resulted in me placing a wall around my heart, designed to protect it from ever being hurt again. Dennis and I became friends immediately and in February 1972 he finally got the nerve to ask me out on a date. After a few months of dating, our unmet needs to feel love from our parents were so great, we chose to enter a place in our relationship that was forbidden by God outside of marriage. And so by September 1972 we were married and expecting our first child. I was fifteen and had to quit school. Dennis was seventeen. Because he was a senior in high school, we decided he would continue schooling so he could graduate.

The early part of our marriage was at the same time wonderful and awful. Initially things were good; I was happy playing the little housewife as we worked at becoming a family. Dennis would go to school and work, then come home to me and our son.

But slowly times began to change. The pressures of being teenagers in adult roles began affecting our relationship. Tension and fighting became the norm for our household. Some small thing. . .anything. . .would set me off on an angry tirade, and Dennis would spend the next few hours trying to reconcile with me. I had no control of my temper or my selfishness. Deep inside I knew that I was behaving badly, but I didn't know how else to be. I was handling my problems just the way I'd seen my parents handle theirs. I really wanted "us" to be healthy, but I had no clue what that really meant or how to accomplish that.

Dennis seemed able to be much more loving and kind than I. He seemed to have something I didn't. Even though he was reluctant to talk about his faith, over time I learned that what he *had* was Christ. I wasn't really sure what it meant to *have* Christ, but I determined if that's what helped Dennis be the kind of person he was, then I wanted it, too.

After hearing my father-in-law preach a fire-and-brimstone sermon at a revival service, I accepted Jesus as my Savior. I didn't realize it at the time, but I was more scared out of hell than loved into heaven. Since grace was not part of the messages being given, I didn't understand just how this Savior could change my life, but I figured that finally I could be the kind of person I wanted to be, and Dennis and I could live happily ever after. I guess I expected God would wave His magic wand over me, somehow transforming me into a different person.

Sadly, that's not exactly what happened. All of a sudden, people were telling me how I should act, look, think, and talk as a Christian. I responded by trying to do and be all those things. And I managed nicely for awhile. But as we had more children, the pressures of raising a family and keeping up the façade of being nice "Suzy Christian" piled up. I began to lose what small grip I had on my self-control. I just couldn't deal with the enormous stress of being a twenty-two-year-old wife and mother to four children.

As our children grew, my uncontrollable anger began to pour out on them as well as on Dennis. I knew I was causing deep hurt to this man and these children that I loved, but I didn't know how else to be. I became very frightened, knowing something had to change.

I tried talking with other Christian women, hoping that if I shared my struggles while trying to be the godly woman in Proverbs 31, they might have some suggestions for me. Most often these women would respond with what seemed to me a pat answer and then tell me that I was just being too hard on myself. They'd say I was expecting too much from my marriage, from being a Christian, and so on. They'd remind me that everyone has troubles. But they hadn't seen me throw that quart of peaches at Dennis while in a rage. They didn't know about the time I followed him up the street, pounding his back because he was trying to walk out of an argument. They didn't know about the vicious arguments that would last most of the night. We'd managed to keep our dirty little secret just that—secret. No one knew the real trouble our marriage and family were in.

The longer we were married, the worse things got. We didn't believe in divorce, but we knew things couldn't continue this way either. Something had to give. Finally, I came across a set of books on the marriage relationship written by Gary Smalley. I read them and realized there was a lot I had to learn about my husband and being a godly wife. . .more than I'd ever anticipated when I married. But I was willing to learn. I believed that if I could just master the "ten steps to a happy marriage," then we could finally live the kind of life I wanted for us.

I asked Dennis to read the books, too. He hates to read but was willing to do anything to try to make "us" better. It was while he was reading through the "husband's" book that God revealed to him that I wasn't the only one who needed "fixing." God showed Dennis that he had a lot to learn about relating to me. Dennis realized that the way he dealt with anger wasn't healthy and that he struggled with other areas, too. Pride and arrogance came through not as much in his actions as in his thoughts. He believed I was the problem and treated me as such. Dennis learned that there were definitely things he needed to change, and so he set about trying to make those changes.

Eventually, God showed Dennis something that wasn't in the book, something he didn't expect at all. God showed him the biggest change that needed to be made had nothing to do with me or with how he related to me. God revealed that the biggest issue in Dennis's life needing to be addressed was that he had taken God off His rightful place on the throne of his heart and had placed our marriage and me there. Dennis had spent so much time trying to "fix" me that he had neglected his own issues. God showed him that it wasn't *his* job to try to make me into the great little Christian wife. Instead, he should allow God to deal with me while Dennis worked on his own weaknesses.

As for me, well, I did pretty good at following the steps mentioned in those books. . .for awhile. . .and as long as nothing too difficult would enter our lives. But once a crisis came along, I would revert to my "old self," responding to the stress just the way I always had. . .with an angry outburst. My being a Christian didn't seem to help me during those times. I just didn't know what else to do. I'd read the Bible and all the books on marriage I could find. I'd prayed the prayers people told me to, and I'd talked with mature Christians 'til I was blue in the face. Still, I just couldn't seem to make the necessary changes that would take us emotionally intact through those crises.

Our children were rebelling, and Dennis and I seemed further away from each other than ever before. I felt like I was drowning in hopelessness. I didn't know what to do, but I did know that something more than what I had was needed.

One night, as the impossibility of our situation overwhelmed me, I was lying prostrate on the floor, weeping into the carpet. I remember thinking, *If this is all there is to being a Christian, then I might as well pull the trigger right now, because this just isn't enough! I can't do this anymore.* I screamed at God that if I was going to make it as a wife, as a mother, or even as a Christian, then He was just going to have to change me Himself, because I was too tired to try anymore. I told Him that if there is more to this faith walk, then He had better show me what it was, and soon, or I was checking out of life. I was somewhat less than reverent in my demands.

God in His mercy responded to my tearful demands. That night, lying facedown on my floor, exhausted and completely spent from weeping, I felt the quiet, gentle presence of Christ next to me. I sensed rather than heard Jesus tell me that there was more and that He'd been trying to tell me that in a number of ways. He told me that I had not been listening. Gently, Jesus reminded me that I'd not really handed my problems over to Him. Instead of giving my problems to Him and trusting Him to do things His way, I'd gripped my marriage, my children, and my life tightly in my own hands, attempting to solve problems in my own strength. Oh, I'd done the "steps," I'd read the Bible, I'd even prayed the prayers; but I'd never really given up control.

I knew He was right about me. When I was saved, I expected Jesus to take control of my life and direct it as one does with a remote control car. When He didn't just take control and wave His magic wand over me, turning me into a Christian version of Betty Crocker, Martha Stewart, and June Cleaver all rolled into one, I took things into my own hands and "did it my way." I had tried so hard to change myself without realizing that my efforts were doomed to failure from the beginning!

That night, right there on the floor, I felt something (or perhaps I should say *Someone*) enter my heart and permeate my entire being. In desperation, I released my grip on my life and family, and God poured His Holy Spirit into me, and over time He began to "fix" me. As I allowed the Spirit access to my deepest heart of hearts, He ever so gently scoured away the scar tissue that had formed over its many wounds. Wounds from the abuse and pain inflicted when I was a little girl. Wounds from the terrible choices I'd made over the years. Wounds from the fights Dennis and I'd had.

As the Holy Spirit healed my wounds, the anger that I'd stuffed down for so many years began to dissipate. I stopped responding to Dennis and the children with the fury that had once consumed me. Slowly, love began to replace the anger, and I became someone entirely different from the woman that Dennis had married.

The Holy Spirit began to teach me what all those things I'd read in the Bible over the years meant. Those things about placing Jesus in the position of Lord of my life—not just Savior. Those things about being transformed into the image of Christ. Those things about dying to my flesh and walking in the Spirit. As I yielded control to Him, He began accomplishing in me all those things that I had unsuccessfully tried so hard to do.

It's been about fifteen years since I spent that night on the carpet experiencing the beginning of a restoration process. A lot has happened during the in-between years. Dennis continued allowing God to change him. . .and me, too! God has graciously and continually renewed our love for each other and for Him as well. Instead of being separate and frustrated with each other, Dennis and I have grown so close that we no longer know where one ends and the other begins. Our relationship isn't perfect and neither are we. While it took us a very long time to realize it, we now know that we are not perfect in and of ourselves. . . but we are perfect for each other. We've learned that the very best thing we can do to have a thriving marriage is to focus on Christ and not each other, to follow wherever He leads, and to allow Him access to the deepest part of our hearts. When we do that, He prompts our hearts toward each other in wonderful ways. Ways that are designed to strengthen and renew our love for each other and for the King of Kings.

In short, we've learned the best route to attaining a growing and healthy marriage is to place Jesus Christ on the throne of our hearts, allow the Holy Spirit complete control of our lives, and, of course, place the "fixing" of what is wrong in the other into the hands of the King.

We've learned, too, that Jesus Christ as Savior is wonderful, but Jesus Christ as Lord of our lives has the power to transform what is broken into wholeness, sadness into joy, and, praise God, those who are two into one.

TINA SHUMAN

Dennis and Tina's Precious Verse:

The LORD is a refuge for the oppressed, a stronghold in times of trouble. Those who know your name will trust in you, for you, LORD, have never forsaken those who seek you.

PSALM 9:9–10

Immature love says: "I love you because I need you."
Mature love says: "I need you because I love you."

ERICH FROMM

If ever two were one, then surely we.
If ever man were loved by wife, then thee.

ANNE BRADSTREET

Dante and I are best friends; we have open communication with each other. We talk about everything. There is nothing I can't take to him; whether I have good news, bad news, when I am happy, and when I am sad. He loves me the way God loves me, unconditionally. He is my rock, my stabling factor, and my hero. He is the answer to my prayers. We have like interests. We love to go camping, hiking, fishing, and do things as a family. We are both artistic. I do ceramics and he is a wonderful photographer. He plays the guitar and I sing. We complement each other's gifts. We do not have a set "date night," but we do go out on a date about once every month. I am not saying that it has all been peaches and cream. We have had some scary times; but we always talk things out, and I think that is how we have stayed best friends. We pray for each other and we pray for the children. We believe marriage is a sacrament, a gift from God. It must be treated as such. It is like the life of a newborn; it has to be taken care of so it can grow into a lasting relationship. If you take the time to care for your marriage as you would a newborn, then it will grow and become such a strong bond that you will not be able to tell where one person starts and the other finishes.

SHERRY MORRISON MISENCIK,
Married August 31, 1984

Angel's feathers †

Emmitt and Joan Clayton

In their forty-plus years of marriage, it has been Emmitt's faith that sustained his and Joan's marriage. It has been Emmitt who has been the strong one when the storms of life blow against the windowpanes of their love. And 1980 was no exception.

Joan and a family member had a misunderstanding of such proportions it seemed the entire family was shattered. It seemed to Joan that her heart would break; peace was nowhere to be found.

"Let it go!" Emmitt said, time and again. "You're making yourself sick, and there's no sense in that, Joan. It isn't worth it! We've prayed about it and that's all we can do."

One night, after a week of emotional agony, Emmitt rushed an exhausted and dehydrated Joan to the emergency room. After he brought her home, he held her close and said, "I love you more than anything. You are my life! Don't let this throw you!"

Joan tossed and turned in bed as Emmitt slept beside her. She watched in misery as the numbers on her digital clock clicked off the time, and she reflected on the look of pain in Emmitt's eyes earlier in the night. Finally, as the darkness of night gave way to the wee hours of the morning, Joan looked over at her husband. *How can he sleep?* she wondered. *The minute his head hits the pillow, he starts snoring!*

Eventually, sleep came. When Joan awoke a few hours later, she expected the continued sadness to be tinged with grogginess. Unexpectedly, total peace surrounded her!

Even Joan's attempts to be anxious didn't work! She tried to worry and couldn't. As she busied herself with her daily tasks, she took a crack at being upset but couldn't muster even that.

That evening, as she stood wrapped in the warm embrace of her husband, she confided, "As far as I know, nothing has changed. The situation is the same as it's been for awhile. But today I was covered with a blanket of peace. I am no longer anxious. I feel like God is in control and I can completely let go of it." Joan shook her head slightly. "I just can't understand it."

"Honey," Emmitt whispered as he held her close, "I was praying last night about the situation, and as I was drifting off to sleep, the most wonderful thing happened. Maybe it was a dream. I don't know. But I do know what I saw. From far off, a beautiful being, dressed in white, came to my side of the bed. He was the most beautiful being. I can see it now in my mind's eye. As soon as I can, I'm going to paint what I saw." (Emmitt is an artist.)

"When the being stopped at my side of the bed, he then covered us with beautiful white feathers. They just unfolded and rippled over us, covering us completely with those huge, soft, fluffy feathers." Emmitt's voice began to break as tears began to slip down his cheeks.

"Emmitt, you are my life! There's no doubt in my mind that your prayers and God's intervention saved me! I am so thankful for you. You are God's gift to me. I know, without a doubt, that God made you just for me, to watch over, love, and protect me.

I can never thank the Lord enough, Emmitt. Never!"

The following Sunday, while waiting for church services to begin, Joan randomly opened her Bible. As her eyes gazed upon the passage near her fingertips, she gasped.

He will cover you with his feathers, and under his wings you will find refuge. PSALM 91:4

Emmitt and Joan's Precious Verse:

" 'Call to me and I will answer you and tell you great and unsearchable things you do not know.' " JEREMIAH 33:3

We seek the comfort of another. Someone to share, and share the life we choose. Someone to help us through the never-ending attempt to understand ourselves. And in the end, someone to comfort us along the way.

MARLIN FINCH LUPUS

We'd been married seven years when the defining moment in our marriage occurred. I functioned as a homemaker, spending mindless days with our two young children, Darcy and Mark. Larry seemed to prefer to spend as many hours as possible at work. One morning, as casual as an old, blue cardigan, Larry announced, "I'm flying to San Jose for the day." I quickly suggested that the kids and I go with him. "Kathy, I'm sorry," he said. "You can't go because I only rented a two-seater plane and I've already asked Joe to go." I was bordering on furious when he walked out the door leading to our garage. When he closed it soundly behind him, I looked down at my hand. There, in a tight fist, was the half-eaten apple I'd been enjoying just five minutes ago. A surge of anger boiled up within me, and I threw the apple with all my strength at the closed door. The apple shattered, spraying pieces across the ceiling and walls.

For months, I watched the pieces of shattered apple as they turned brown and began to rot. In my mind, they represented my shattered marriage. . .a marriage that just seven years ago held such promise. But eventually I realized how wrong I was; Larry couldn't meet all my needs. Only God could. I turned to Him and began to experience the full power of His love and acceptance.

I soon found a book by Tim LaHaye, *Understanding the Male Temperament.* I wanted to understand my husband, so I began to read, captivated by what I learned. I realized he and I saw life from different viewpoints, which was okay! As I continued to study and pray, I began to surrender myself completely to what God expected from me as Larry's wife. And I knew my first act was to wash the rotting apple pieces from the ceiling and walls. In doing so I was saying, "Larry, I release you from the unrealistic expectations I have placed on you. I choose to love you unconditionally. I am set free!"

KATHY COLLARD MILLER
(Kathy and Larry are the authors of
When the Honeymoon's Over [Shaw, 1997] and
What's in the Bible for Couples [Starburst, 2001].)

One True Vow

Larry and Kathy's Precious Verse:

A gentle answer turns away wrath, but a harsh word stirs up anger.   PROVERBS 15:1

Kind words can be short and easy to speak, but their echoes are truly endless.

MOTHER TERESA

The day we married, my husband presented me with two very special gifts: my stepchildren, Christopher, age eight, and Ashley, age two. For over twenty-two years I have loved my precious gifts with an abandoned heart. They know I would lay down my life for either one of them. But as much as I adore them, my desire is that they *not* enter into a blended family. *Why?* It is because marriage is difficult enough without bringing ex or deceased spouses into it. A man can only be married to one woman at a time, and vice versa. I was blessed with a husband who stood beside me 100 percent of the time. No one was allowed to say "You're not my real mother!" or challenge my authority in the home.

"How can you take her side over mine? I'm your son!" my stepson—a teenager at the time—questioned his father one evening.

My husband replied calmly, "Because when you leave this home one day and take a wife of your own, she is the one who will still be with me."

I was blessed; I know many couples in like situations whose homes look like a battlefield with two distinct sides. . .his family and her family. This breaks my heart.

When I first married and the trials of joining a ready-made family occurred, I turned to the Word of God for guidance. I searched and I searched! I found nothing. . .*absolutely nothing*. . . which began: *"And the Lord said, 'When your husband's ex-wife says to you. . .' "*, or: *"When your wife's children reject your authority. . . ."* There was nothing about visitation rights, balancing a budget when the top of the list reads: child support, bringing your first child into a family of four, et cetera. (I often said that one day my daughter would write a book titled *My Sister Was an Only Child*.)

One day, as I continued this scriptural scavenger hunt, it dawned on me that God had placed no specifics on these issues because these issues were never in His plan. Aha! What I would have to do, I decided, would be to study the principles of godliness, kindness, peace, love, forgiveness, and so forth; and apply them to the situation. Sometimes this was easy; other times this was difficult. . .at best.

We survived it all, just as any family with children survives the ups and downs of two parents raising distinct, individual children. But it was hard. . .it was really, really hard. And so my preference was that my children not marry into ready-made families.

Well, guess what? As it happened, my stepson married a young woman with an adorable son and is as happy as a clam, if you will pardon the cliché. Chances are good that my girls will marry into blended families. I know it's not ideal, but with God, it can work!

EVA MARIE EVERSON

Raising kids is part joy and part guerrilla warfare.

ED ASNER

David and I made a decision a long time ago as to what's really important. The things that last a lifetime are our marriage and our kids. We're very careful not to place anyone or anything above them.

ROBI LIPSCOMB,
Married August 13, 1983

Then Peter came to Jesus and asked,
"Lord, how many times shall I forgive my brother
when he sins against me? Up to seven times?"
Jesus answered, "I tell you, not seven times,
but seventy-seven times."

MATTHEW 18:21–22

When Don asked me to marry him, my fourteen-year-old daughter, Jana, was ecstatic. She even commented that she'd like for Don to adopt her. We gave her everything: a queen-sized water bed she begged us to buy, her own stereo system, a color television, her own phone line, clothes, and all the privacy she could ever need. Jana had survived a terrible trauma; and I suppose that, in our own way, we were trying to make life a little better. You see, sometime earlier, my ex-husband had taken Jana's brother and me hostage, resulting in the shooting death of our son by his father. At the end of this nightmare, Jana's father was arrested and incarcerated. It was a hard time for all of us, and we wanted to smooth it over as best we could, to give her some sense of normalcy.

But within a short time she became restless. We began to argue; she said that I didn't care about her. . .didn't include her in any of my plans. She felt betrayed, she said. Abandoned again. I felt as though she was refusing me the right to ever be happy after my abusive marriage to her father. It was truly awful, but Don and I formed a united front in our efforts to reach her.

My daughter and I began therapy, but things didn't get any better at home. Suddenly I was hearing things like, "You're not my father and I don't have to do anything you say!" This, of course, would lead to me becoming angry, retaliating with phrases like, "As long as you live in Don's house and he is paying the bills, you will respect him!"

But our marriage was threatened when we began to argue about Jana. I was torn between my loyalty to my daughter, who had just experienced the worse kind of traumatic event in her life, and my new husband. Sometimes I felt he was too strict toward her and other times not strict enough. He complained about having to live with Jana and her teenage demands and selfishness. He said it ate at him day in and day out. His son, he said, never got away with the stuff Jana got away with. . .he made his son toe the mark. Sometimes I felt offended when he said things about Jana. "She won't do her chores," he said. "She's selfish and wants us to do everything for her and to buy her things, then takes advantage of us. She only thinks about herself and no one else." At the time, these things were true, but I was still offended by his remarks.

It wasn't that we fought all the time. There were a few hot and heavy arguments about her, but those were few and far between. All in all, Don and I were united in our stand. Still, at times I thought about just moving into my own apartment with Jana and raising her alone (Jana, of course, would have loved that). In my heart I thought I would be allowing Don to be free to find someone who would make him happy, someone who would give him a stress-free, teenage-free life. The perfect woman. . .a woman whose life would revolve around him alone and not be preoccupied with a teenage daughter. . .a woman who lived a normal life and didn't have such a violent and tragic past.

Don began having some colon and stomach problems (due to stress) and was admitted to the hospital for several days. At that time I felt incredibly guilty. I went as far as telling him our marriage wasn't working out and I needed to leave to "set him free to find his perfect woman or to ask his ex-wife to come home."

Don became angry! He retaliated by saying I wanted to "abandon him during his weakest moment"! I cried and he assured me how much he loved me and how much he wanted me to stay. He said he needed me and that there was no other perfect woman in the world for him but me. I, too, told him I loved him and couldn't live without him.

Jana got involved with a man over twenty-one years of age and ran away from home to live with him and his father. When Don and I threatened to have charges brought up against him, Jana moved out but didn't return home. Rather, she went to live with a girlfriend.

In spite of the agony of not knowing if my daughter was okay, Don and I became closer after Jana was out of the house. As various issues concerning my daughter came up, he and I remained a united front. I suppose you could say that Don became my ally!

He advised me on how to handle her and stopped me from making dumb, rash decisions, and I stayed "on my knees" constantly.

Soon, Jana began to come to us with her problems and worries. She found Don very easy to talk to, wise, and intuitive. She came to depend on his advice. The day finally came when we sat in the grandstands to watch Jana graduate from high school. She matured into an intelligent, beautiful woman with a bright and successful future. A year later we orchestrated her wedding. Today, she and her husband are the strong Christian parents of our grandchildren.

Don and I survived extreme hardships early in our marriage, but it made us stronger, both as individuals and as a couple. In spite of the difficulties, we are so much better for having lived through them.

SUSAN J. SHELLEY

Don and Susan's Precious Verse:

> *But I will sing of your strength, in the morning I will sing of your love; for you are my fortress, my refuge in times of trouble.*　　　PSALM 59:16

My husband doesn't like that I travel. However, traveling has been a part of my life for all my adult years. When I met him, I was teaching seminars all over the country, so I think he'd have grown accustomed to this after so many years of marriage. Instead he likes it less and less.

Returning home via plane, I often enjoy the relaxing escape

of a good romance novel. As I read, I picture Chuck meeting me at the gate with roses in his hand. Instead, I deplane and walk alone through the terminal, get my baggage, and go to my car. I wait in line to pay for my parking and drive home. Because I like to get home from a trip as soon as possible, I frequently arrive late at night rather than the next day. Therefore, Chuck is often asleep when I get home. I tiptoe in, drop my bags, and undress in the dark. I crawl into bed beside him, and he wiggles his foot against my leg to welcome me home. This is hardly the romance novel scene I had painted in my mind.

Recently, a scheduled trip had me flying home the day after a seminar, which was also the day of our sixteenth anniversary. Since it was our anniversary, I really wanted that romance novel scene. The day before, I had arranged to have flowers sent to his office with a card that said "Happy Anniversary! Hurry home!" (I had the flowers delivered in the morning in case he forgot what day it was. They would remind him and he'd have time to do whatever he needed to do.) I planned to arrive home before he got off work. I had time to shop for the ingredients to make a lovely dinner. I arrived home, prepared dinner, and put it all aside. I went into the bedroom and found something small and black hanging on our four-poster bed with an anniversary card. (He hadn't forgotten after all.) I relaxed in a bubble bath and put my present on. I lit candles in the bedroom. It was nearly time for him to arrive. I curled up on the bed and read my romance novel. I waited. The dogs barked and I heard his car door. I tucked the romance novel away and placed myself artfully across the bed.

Today, I could write a romance novel with the results of my efforts!

Since I had sent Chuck flowers, he knew that I had not forgotten what day it was. He knew I'd be waiting and he knew what he had waiting for me. He was excited to see me; glad I had come home. While the night left me breathless, I thought it through in the morning. That was the reaction I'd like every time I get home!

I thought, *What can I change that would bring about the desired effect?* First, I could change my schedule so I arrive home before he does. I can fix a special dinner. I can put on one of the many "little somethings" he has given me over the years that I know he likes, and I can place myself across the bed as if in a lingerie catalog. Yes, I can do that.

My next trip I put this plan to action. It worked again— even without the special day or the flowers. My next trip I tried it again. It worked again! I had created an attitude adjustment. While he is still not crazy about my traveling, he loves my coming home. Without travel, I wouldn't be putting forth the homecoming effort. Maybe travel isn't so bad after all. . . .

MARITA LITTAUER
(Marita Littauer and husband, Chuck Noon,
are the authors of *Love Extravagantly,*
[Bethany, 2001].)

Chuck and Marita's Precious Verse:

If it is possible, as far as it depends on you, live at peace with everyone. ROMANS 12:18

As women, we don't just take all we can take. We have to give all we can give. BECKY HUNTER

I learned what it meant to love CeCe
the way Christ loved the church.
Jesus stands by us no matter
how stubborn or disobedient we've been. . . .
I looked back and realized God's grace in my life—
where I've come from and
what He's blessed me with in CeCe.

ALVIN LOVE

If love were what the rose is,
And I were like the leaf,
Our lives would grow together
In sad or singing weather.

ALGERNON CHARLES SWINBURNE

Anniversary Gifts

ANNIVERSARY	TRADITIONAL	MODERN
First	Paper	Clock
Second	Cotton	China
Third	Leather	Crystal/Glass
Fourth	Flowers	Appliances
Fifth	Wood	Silverware
Sixth	Candy/Iron	Wood
Seventh	Wood/Copper	Desk Sets
Eighth	Bronze/Pottery	Linens/Lace
Ninth	Pottery/Willow	Leather
Tenth	Tin/Aluminum	Diamond Jewelry
Eleventh	Steel	Fashion Jewelry
Twelfth	Silk/Linen	Pearls
Thirteenth	Lace	Textiles/Furs
Fourteenth	Ivory	Gold Jewelry
Fifteenth	Crystal	Watches
Twentieth	China	Platinum
Twenty-fifth	Silver	Silver
Thirtieth	Pearl	Diamond
Thirty-fifth	Coral	Jade
Fortieth	Ruby	Ruby
Forty-fifth	Sapphire	Sapphire
Fiftieth	Gold	Gold
Fifty-fifth	Emerald	Emerald
Sixtieth	Diamond	Diamond

For Richer. . .
For Poorer. . .

Happy couples make five times as many deposits as withdrawals into their relationship. Deposits are positive experiences that provide your mate energy and security. A gentle touch, a listening ear, a hug, or a verbal "I love you" are just a few examples on a long list.

GARY SMALLEY

*I*ntimacy is working alongside somebody.

Dr. Joel Hunter

*W*hen we had a conflict over finances or a disappointment over failed expectations, I realized that I should take the first step to confess my wrong and make things right. Pride builds walls of self-protection, but love seeks to be reconciled.

Steve Green

I spotted the grasshopper on an outside window ledge. Throughout the morning I watched him, basking in the warm sunshine, his wings periodically quivering in the gentle breeze. Near noon, as the January wind started to increase, the grasshopper stirred from his resting place. As he inched his way up the tempered glass, I noticed that one of his back legs was missing. His antennae worked furiously, guiding him. Inch by inch, push by push, with only five legs and the wind force against him, he finally reached his goal. A while later, satisfied with his victory, I watched as he returned to the ledge.

I was immediately reminded of a time, six years earlier, when we'd moved to Florida to take advantage of a business opportunity for my husband. At the time of the move, we considered it a most wonderful gift from God. Now, it seemed a curse from the enemy. Eight months later, my husband and

I stared at a letter informing us that we had placed our "faith" in a farce. In a moment that is difficult to describe, our lives changed forever, as did our social position. We went from having the world by the tail to imminent danger of watching everything we'd worked for slip through our fingers.

In all honesty, I don't think we truly realized the full impact of the situation. Within months, our savings was drained. We were forced to cash in our life insurance policies and IRAs. We sold some of our possessions and moved into a small, two-bedroom apartment with a fraction of the space we'd had a year earlier. We even filed for bankruptcy, hoping it would help to get us back on our feet. And finally, in our darkest hour, we requested governmental assistance in the form of welfare and food stamps.

The minutes in each day stretched into hours and days of unending listlessness, like on hot, humid summer afternoons when you're keenly aware of every breath that you take. Sometimes it was I who was the strong one; some days it was my husband.

My husband and I had always been the "givers." I'm not speaking just in terms of tithing, but in giving to others, the needy. Previously, I'd assumed that receiving a gift was easy. It's not. It's uncomfortably humbling. There were many days when I walked to our mailbox, praying to God about how we were going to pay the rent or the electric bill. I'd nearly collapse to my knees when I'd find an unexpected check, given to help us meet our needs. There were times when I stood before the open refrigerator, staring into its white barrenness and praying, "Lord, exactly what are the plans for dinner tonight? We have no food. Yet, You said Your seed would never be forsaken or beg for bread. What would You have me do here?" Often, before I could close the refrigerator door, the phone would ring. "Just wanted to see if you were free for dinner tonight. We're buying." It happened time and again.

With all the miracles—too numerous to list in this limited space—there is one that stands above them all: the miracle that took place inside my heart. Never had I clung to the Word of God as I did during that trial. Never had I felt His comforting hand on my shoulder as I felt it then. I felt His wisdom growing inside of me, forming me into what He had always desired for me. The defining moment came one brisk, winter morning. Weeks earlier, I'd seen an outfit in a boutique window that just had my name all over it. Oh, how I wanted it! It was *me!* A year earlier, I'd have bought it and thought nothing of it. But now, I didn't have enough to shop at a thrift store, much less an upscale boutique. That morning I saw my husband's ex-business partner's wife wearing the outfit. I cried all the way home, begging God to explain this to me. "Isn't it enough that I'm down on my knees? Does life have to kick me in the gut, too?" I cried in agony.

I nearly ran into our apartment. As I bolted the door behind me, the phone rang. It was my dear, dear friend, Donald. "Hey, Honey," he greeted me in his usual way. "Listen, I don't know why. . .but God has impressed on me to tell you this. It doesn't matter what you drive, where you live, how much money you have, or what clothes you wear. What matters is that you trust Him."

This was more than just a moment of truth for me. It was the moment that would change my viewpoint on our situation. Donald received a message meant for him to give to me, and he followed through with what God told him to do. It was the message I needed to change my heart. From that moment, wounded and battered like the grasshopper, I turned my faith upward and began the road toward perfection. As God began to work on this wounded heart, I found I was more capable of being a "helpmeet" to my husband as he struggled with our situation. My prayers began to focus more on his needs rather my wants, on his fears rather than my frustrations. When my husband took on the attitude of defeat, I didn't whine with him. . .I kicked him in the seat of the pants (so to speak). And when his faith wavered, I grabbed his hands and said, "No! God won't let us down! Let's pray right now!" In the middle of the storm, we held a sturdier grip on our faith, growing closer to each other and to the awesome God we serve.

EVA MARIE EVERSON

When all of this—
all the glitz and glory and fame—is gone,
you have nothing if you have no one to share it with.

FAITH HILL

We lived away from our families during the first few years of our marriage, and I believe this helped a lot. We depended on each other for everything. All in all, it's a lot of give and take. Some days I give and some days I take. For example, we enjoy doing a lot of things together even though we are complete opposites. Jim loves to fish and I love just being in the boat reading a book. I love to go, and Jim loves to stay at home, but sometimes he goes places with me that I know he really doesn't want to. That's all part of the give and take. We always go to church together, and I believe that the family that prays together stays together. Life is one day at a time, and we just have to live it as such. Jim is my helper and friend; and I look forward to the next twenty-two years, or whatever God gives us.

JEANETTE B. BRUNER,
Married May 27, 1978

*Two souls with but a single thought,
two hearts that beat as one...*

JOHN KEATS

Did He? Would He?

Chris and Sue Maakestad

Sue Maakestad sat at the kitchen table in the mobile home she shared with her husband, Chris, and their eight children. Spread out before her were stacks of bills, both household and medical, most of which were printed in red ink. Past Due. Remit Immediately. Due upon Receipt. While her children played, her husband rested in the bedroom, recuperating from brain surgery. And Sue played "One Potato, Two Potato" with the bills. It violated everything Chris had taught her about finances, but the disability income was barely enough to make ends meet. Each creditor got a little something each month. Usually.

Six months earlier, in late 1984, Chris had begun to complain of headaches and exhaustion.

"Well, of course you're exhausted, Babe," Sue said. "The move to Tucson took nearly everything out of you! You set the trailer up yourself. You dug trenches for all the utility lines that didn't even exist. You've single-handedly taken on the water company, making them come out here to set the meter!"

"But we don't even have electric and gas yet," Chris said. "Not even a telephone."

"We will soon. I'm sure all this has been a key factor in your headaches and all."

Chris accepted the explanation halfheartedly. Sue returned shortly and found her husband asleep in the middle of the living room floor. Nudging him awake, she said, "Maybe you should see a doctor, Babe."

"A doctor. Right. Who do you want me to see? We don't know any doctors up here. Besides, I don't need a doctor. You're probably right. It's just the move."

A week later, they knew it had to be much more serious than that.

"When the phone rings at work, I get a flash across my eyes," Chris told his wife. "If I look at your face, I see pieces missing like a puzzle," he continued. "When I look at a straight line, I see notches in it."

"That's it! You're going to a doctor!"

Sue compiled a list of physicians from the local yellow pages. Chris said he would call them from his job. After several days had gone by, Sue confiscated the unused list and set an appointment for him.

Two weeks passed. The gas and electric had been turned on. Broke from the move, Chris and Sue put off getting a phone for awhile.

Early on the morning of Chris's appointment, the oldest children were doing chores around the house while Sue finished nursing the baby. Chris ambled down the hall, looking handsome and serious.

"Come with me," he said. Sue followed him to the sofa, their only piece of living room furniture. "The doctor isn't just going to write me a prescription and send me home," he began.

"Why not? How do you know? It's just a doctor's appointment, Babe."

"I think what I have isn't that easy to fix."

"Don't say that. You're going to be fine."

"I'm just telling you," he said.

Sue stopped arguing. There was something in her husband's eyes. . .something that registered truth to her heart and mind. She nodded.

"Before you go, let's pray."

They did. Chris left.

He didn't return.

An hour later, Sue opened her front door to find their Bible study leader, Cheryon Unruh, and her oldest daughter, Valerie, standing beside her.

"They called me to come bring you to the hospital," she said. "Valerie's here. She can stay with the kids."

"Where's Chris? Is he in the hospital? Why? What's happening?"

"He's okay. He'll give you the lowdown when we get there," she said. "I know nothing. I'm just the taxi."

A while later, Sue stood over her husband's hospital bed. "What's going on here?" she asked.

"The doctor wouldn't let me go home," he said.

"Yeah, I can see that. He's got a lot of nerve."

"Actually, it wasn't the first doctor you made the appointment with. That guy just yelled at me and said I didn't need an ear doctor; I needed my head examined."

"Very funny."

"No, really. He sent me to a neurologist. It's amazing he could find anybody. It was after five o'clock already, and he called around and found this guy right across the street still hanging around his office."

"That was God."

"Yeah. And I went to the other guy and he cussed me up one side and down the other and told me I should be dead already and would have been if I had waited another week. He had a real mouth on him."

"That was God, too."

"Yeah, right. I don't think so."

"Well, I do. God had to find somebody who would tell it like it is. You still wouldn't even have made an appointment if I left it up to you. So how did he know all that? Did he do a CAT scan or something?"

"No. I told him my symptoms and he told me it was obvious. He said he didn't need a *blankety-blank* CAT scan to know I have a huge tumor growing in my brain. But it's not malignant," he said quickly, noting the alarm on Sue's face.

"Oh, yeah? Well, then, what's all this about a week and everything?"

"Because it's so big, it's pushing everything inside my head out of the way. But the skull doesn't give it room to be pushed. When he looked at my retina, all he could see was hemorrhage. It's pressing everything against the back of my eyes. That's why they stuffed me in here so quick. They have to do something immediately. They want to do it tomorrow morning."

"Do what? Take it out?"

"No, they have to relieve the pressure first with something called a shunt, or I'll go blind from the pressure."

"Great! So they're *not* going to remove it?"

"They will, but they have to do the shunt first and let it heal."

"So, how long are they keeping you in here, then?" Sue's eyes began to tear.

"I'll be here for awhile, I guess. Listen; we'll know more after tomorrow. Okay?"

Sue nodded in agreement, but her heart screamed, *No! It's not okay!*

The following morning's test revealed a tumor the size of an orange. The operation didn't last long, and by that evening Chris was sitting up, eating dinner. Sue was relieved. It looked as if everything was going to be just fine.

"Honey," Chris said, interrupting her reverie, "you need to bring all the financial papers and budgets and checkbooks to me when you come here tomorrow. I have to teach you everything in a hurry."

"What? Why? What do you mean? I *can't* do that! You've always done all that."

"Look, I won't be able to do it for awhile. I should have taught you all this stuff a long time ago."

Sue sat back in the standard hospital visitor's chair and tried to digest what Chris was saying. She didn't want to learn how to run the house! That was Chris's job! He even did the shopping while she stayed home, relishing her peace in blissful ignorance. She opened her mouth to protest just as the doctor swept into the room.

"What you have is called an acoustic neuroma," he told Chris flatly.

"So, is that a big, fancy name for a benign tumor?" Sue interrupted.

"Honey, *shhh*," Chris said.

"You don't see too many of these," the doctor continued.

"In fact, I've only seen three in my entire career. We're really pretty inexperienced at this type of tumor removal. We're going to give you a couple of days to heal from today's surgery before we remove the tumor. I have to tell you that the prospects for the outcome aren't bright. In a nutshell, that means if you come through the operation at all, there is a good chance you'll walk with a limp and/or lose the use of the right side of your body."

As the doctor walked out and the couple tried to comprehend what they had just heard, the phone rang. It was Sue's uncle in Nashville. . .the Jewish doctor, his parents' pride and joy. . .but more importantly, the head of neurology at Vanderbilt University. (Raised Jewish, Sue had accepted Jesus as Messiah and Savior while in her teens.)

"Hi, Sweetheart! Who's your doctor?"

Sue gave the name.

"Not familiar. Anybody else?"

Sue gave her uncle the name of the doctor who had "told Chris like it was."

"Don't know him either. So what did they tell you?"

Sue repeated what the doctor had just told them.

"No good," Gerry said. "You need to come out here for the operation. We have a team of guys who've done more than a hundred of them, all successful."

"How can we come out *there?*" Sue questioned realistically. "Okay, wait—I'm sorry, never mind. Let me see what we can do. I'll call you back, okay?"

"He wants us to come to Tennessee," Chris guessed as she hung up.

"Yeah. Where'll we get the money for that? *And what about the kids?* I can't just leave them here. I mean, who would I leave them with, Chris? We don't know anybody in this town!"

"Well, you can't very well take them along."

"Why not? I'll bet kids can go half price. I'm gonna call and find out." Grabbing the Yellow Pages and bedside phone, Sue began to contact airlines. Long minutes later, she waved the white flag. "Seven hundred and fifty dollars round-trip, Chris! No breaks! Full price for anything so much as a hamster that takes up a seat! What a heartless bunch! Who will I leave the kids with, Babe? I can't leave them!"

A gentle knock came at the door. A nurse wearing pink scrubs and a sprinkle of freckles across her nose peeked around the doorway.

"Mrs. Maakestad? You have a call at the nurses' station."

Sue demurred as she followed the nurse. *It's probably Valerie,* she thought. *My kids are probably giving her trouble and she wants me to rescue her.* Sue braced herself as she lifted the receiver.

"Hi, Hon," sang a cheery voice. "Guess what? I'm coming out there tomorrow and you're picking me up."

"What? Who is this? Lydi? That's gotta be you!" Lydia Ross, a dear friend from Tulsa, Oklahoma, was the last voice Sue expected to hear at that moment. Though once very close, she and Lydia hadn't seen each other in nine years.

"Who else? Andy already agreed to keep the kids. God told me three days ago that you needed me, but I couldn't figure out why. Your brother just called and told us about Chris. You can pick me up at the airport at 10 A.M. I'm on United."

"Wait a minute, Lydi—"

"Sorry, Hon," she chirped. "The ticket's nonrefundable. You're stuck with me."

"I'm trying to tell you: We may not even be here. We may be going to Nashville."

"Whatever. You can't take the kids along, you know. I'm your only shot at a twenty-four-hour person. You can't find that in town. People have lives, you know. So, it's United, 10 A.M.

Write it down or you'll forget; I know you."

Sue squared her shoulders and walked back down the hall. She no longer felt guilty for leaving her children behind. She could leave with Chris and know the children were well cared for. As only God could, He had picked the perfect person for the job. But the nagging reality of the $1,500 airfare began to gnaw at her gut. She returned to Chris's room to find her husband's two brothers, Tallak and Peter, and his sister, Martha, and her husband, John, visiting with Chris.

"Chris was just telling us about the surgery and about the two of you going to Nashville," John said.

"What about the kids?" Martha asked. "Do you want them to stay with us in Benson?"

"No, actually that's been taken care of," Sue answered.

"It has?" Chris asked.

"Then you should go. Definitely." Tallak pulled out his wallet and started counting its contents out onto the bed. The other men did the same.

"You guys—" Chris protested.

"Really, people," Sue added.

"Will you guys shut up? I'm counting," John said.

Sue and Chris shut up and watched as the others counted. A quick tally showed $1,500 in cash lying at the foot of the hospital bed.

"Do you always carry around that much cash with you?" Tallak asked.

"No way," John answered. "You?"

"Nope."

"Me either," Peter said. "I just cashed a check. I usually deposit."

"You guys should go. Definitely," said Tallak. "I said that already, huh?"

Martha cried and hugged everyone. Sue picked up the phone and called the airline. A flight was booked. The following day Sue picked Lydia up at the airport and took her to the trailer to show her "the ropes."

"See all these boxes of food and stuff? Chris's company sent them. They took up donations of food and money. So did the church around the corner."

"Is that where you guys go to church?"

"Never darkened their door. A friend of mine goes there. But our church gave us stuff, too. There's enough here to feed two armies."

"That's a good thing," said Lydia. "Even if I had a car, how would I take all these kids shopping with me?"

"I feel so out of control here," Sue confessed in a whisper.

"Well, you are."

"What about my baby? Now I have to quit nursing. . .and the kids and their homeschool studies. . .what about that?"

"There's nothing like the joys of emergency weaning," Lydia said with a grin. "He'll be fine. You're the one that's gonna suffer."

"Thanks, Lydi. I needed that."

"No sweat. And don't worry about the kids. I'll give them their lessons. They'll be totally cared for. Why do you think I came here, anyway?"

"I don't know. Why did you? I can't believe you."

"Because God loves you and He knows you need me here. *That's* why."

"*That's* why? No, that can't be why. I feel like I'm so out of touch with Him right now. I feel like He doesn't think about me at all, right now. How do you know He still loves me?"

"Because He sent *me* here for you. You're His kid. Chris is His kid. Don't you take care of your kids? Don't you think He does?"

"I don't know. Does He? I mean, in theory, I know I'm His

kid and He loves me. But I gotta tell you that I just don't feel it right now. It's not real to me. I mean, in theory, I'm supposed to be God's woman of faith and power, right? Well, in real life, I feel like a limp dishrag! Okay, God sent you here, yes. But you're only here because you listened to Him, not because I did. We have airfare to Nashville, yes. That's because *Chris's* people listened to Him, not *me*. Am I trusting God here? No! I'm so busy worrying about everything and feeling like we're tottering on the brink of disaster here, would I have even heard God? Even if He was speaking to me? I doubt it. And He probably knows better than to try it right now."

"Are you done?"

"And you stand there telling me God still loves me anyway! Right now, I gotta ask myself, *does He?*"

"Yes, He does."

"Why should He? Okay, okay, don't tell me. I get it. I'm His kid. Don't ask why He loves me; just be glad He does. I'm just gonna try to believe that. I'm gonna try real hard."

"There's a lot of people praying for you guys," Lydia said.

"You know, we might be gone for three weeks out there."

"I'm here for six. And you just try to get rid of me."

"You're a doll."

Nashville had a record blizzard the night Chris was admitted to Baptist Hospital, and it lasted the better part of a week. Cars were buried. Flu was rampant. Staffing was at a record low. At 6 A.M. the next morning, Sue kissed him good-bye, he sat up on the gurney and told the nurse about God's love, and they wheeled him out to surgery. Surgery would last all day, so Sue settled in to spend the day praying, stressing, reading her Bible, and asking God to remember them.

Did He? Would He?

Every hour, a nurse from the operating room called with an

update. Sue was grateful but even more grateful for the on-slaught of calls from friends and relatives.

"We're praying for you and Chris," they reminded her. "God loves you and He's going to bring Chris through this okay."

Did He? Would He?

Somewhere in the middle of the day, Sue received the answer as she read her Bible.

> *We know that all things work together for good for those*
> *who love God, who are called according to his purpose.*
>
> ROMANS 8:28 NRSV

The presence of God fell upon the room where Sue waited for her husband's surgery to come to a successful end. All of a sudden, she knew they were smack in the middle of God's will, whether it seemed or felt like it. Sue offered up a prayer of thanks just as Gerry's wife entered the room.

"I just couldn't bring myself to stay away any longer. It's positively indecent for you to be here alone all day."

"Aunt Barbara! I thought you were at work."

"I was. And all day, all I could think about was you sitting here all by yourself."

"I'm fine. And I'm not all by myself. People have been calling me all day."

"Oh, great. Oh, wonderful. That's just what you need at a time like this!"

"Actually, it is. They called to say they're praying for Chris and me. And I got a chance to pray a lot here by myself, too. It's been good for me. I'm okay. God's got everything under control."

"Oh, He does?"

"Yes, He does. Why would He bring us all the way out here if He didn't?"

"But look what time it is already! How long have they had him in there?"

"Fourteen hours."

"Mercy! Fourteen hours! So, what did they say? How's he doing?"

Loud voices and bursts of laughter approached from down the hall. Three men in white lab coats sauntered into the room; they were Chris's team of doctors.

"How's he doing?" Aunt Barbara asked the doctors.

"Who, Chris? Fabulous. Absolutely fabulous!"

"You know that nerve we said we'd have to cut?" one of the doctors asked Sue.

"The one to his mouth?"

"Yes! Well, we didn't have to cut anything."

"Really?" Sue exclaimed. "Thank You, Jesus! And thank you guys, too. You all were great. I really appreciate all you did." She raised her hands and closed her eyes. "Thank You, Jesus! Thank You, Lord!"

For the next three weeks, Sue cared for Chris around the clock. For the first week, he couldn't even ask for a glass of water. Gradually, as he regained use of his body, they hobbled up and down the halls for exercise. His six-foot-five frame leaned heavily on Sue's as the nurses cheered him from the sidelines. Uncle Gerry's prominent status at the university ensured Chris's release into his custody so that the latter part of his recovery could take place in the comfort of his and Barbara's home. It was comfortable, but Chris and Sue were anxious to get back to Tucson. Three weeks later, Chris was approved to step on the plane.

Eight months passed before he was allowed to drive again. Through eight months of disability income, at 60 percent of normal cash flow, their awesome, faithful God provided all the money they needed. They didn't lose their home. Chris's employer held his job. In spite of the hardship, life was good in Jesus.

Sue Maakestad learned some valuable lessons during the trial that her marriage withstood. One, her husband is more precious to her than she ever realized. Two, she knows just how much God truly loves her. Three, if she, as a mother, is so quick to take care of her children, how much more will her heavenly Father take care of His?

Today, unless you're looking for the concave spot behind one ear or the tiny stitch in the corner of one eye, you'd never know Chris Maakestad underwent major brain surgery. He walks with the confident gait of a man who knows the future is in good hands: hands that aren't his own. He's walked two of his daughters down the aisle, and he knows how to enjoy his grand-kids. His sons have followed his steady footsteps in engineering and technology. Best of all, his wife knows how lucky she is. . .and how very blessed.

Chris and Sue's Precious Verse:

The LORD is good, a refuge in times of trouble. He cares for those who trust in him.   NAHUM 1:7

I don't just feel that I married the best man I ever met. I believe that I married the best man there is.

MAVIS (MRS. JAY) LENO

Honor the ocean of love.

GEORGE DE BENNEVILLE

When Jesus Speaks

Tim and Leah Roberts

For some time, Tim and Leah Roberts had become enmeshed in Native American culture. For Tim, a backslidden Christian, it had begun as a mild—but growing—interest. For Leah, a petite, young Jewish woman, it was merely a way of being with her husband. Leah was more interested in astrology and stones. But the more Tim talked about the culture, the more intrigued Leah became. They met a Cherokee woman, Grandmother Sallye, who held monthly Moon Ceremonies and worked with injured birds of prey. Immediately Tim and Leah were in "the circle." In no time, Tim was a spiritual leader—actually preaching at the Moon Ceremonies—and Leah was the worship team leader.

Tim and Leah didn't see any warning signs concerning their new way of life. The Native American spiritual doctrine, *mitakuye oyasin* (we are all one), felt right and comfortable. More than that, it felt real. They began to believe that God was a holy and divine Spirit who lived in everything, animate and inanimate. They accepted the doctrine that said the earth is given to man as his home, therefore God is in all the things of the earth. Worshipping God meant respecting, loving, and caring for all creation.

Short, round Grandmother Sallye had a vision: to gather

the "family" and move to the mountains of North Carolina, where they would set up a commune. Their long-term goal would be to have a facility where abandoned and abused children could come to work with nature and animals and learn to worship God.

"I have other goals," Leah confided to Grandmother Sallye. "I don't want to work with children."

Grandmother Sallye laughed as her black eyes danced. "You are destined to work with children."

Leah frowned. She didn't know about that. . . .

Grandmother Sallye was a dreamer, not an organizer. The plans to move to North Carolina were changed to moving to Tennessee. Tim and Leah were visibly disappointed and said so to their close friends, a couple known as Spring Breeze and Rock Tree.

"I don't like the idea of Tennessee," Tim said.

"We don't either," Rock Tree agreed.

"I'll admit," Leah added, "that I have become disillusioned with a lot of the group and with Grandmother's apparent inability to follow through on her plans."

"Then why don't the four of us, along with our two sons, start our own circle?" Spring Breeze suggested.

"Who gets to tell Grandmother?" Leah asked, half-joking. . . half-not.

"We all will," Tim concluded.

The foursome approached Grandmother Sallye a few days later and received an unexpected reaction. "I'm all for it!" she beamed. "If we are to grow, we must distribute ourselves to others."

Spring Breeze, Rock Tree, Tim, and Leah sold everything they owned to finance their new adventure.

"No income, not much cash for padding, but the way I look at it, our ultimate goal is so pure and good, surely God will bless it," Leah said to Tim.

"We just have to go on faith."

"Not easy when you're a worrywart little Jewish girl," Leah teased, though deep down she was a bit uneasy as to how they were going to make it. But everyone else seemed starry-eyed and convinced, so she took a deep breath and convinced herself, too. "Where will we live?" she asked the group.

"In teepees," Tim answered quickly.

Spring Breeze added, "Rock Tree and I have been doing some research. A good teepee is about $1,400 a pop..."

"They're warm and comfortable," Rock Tree interjected.

"...and as far as homes go, $1,400 is a bargain!"

Tim added, "We have to find a piece of property before we move."

"It must be completely remote," Rock Tree said. "No neighbors, good soil, and large enough to provide a home for the commune we will eventually have."

"I think the four of us should go up to North Carolina and check out the area," Tim suggested.

"Agreed," the others said.

Just when it came time for the scheduled trip to find land, Leah's mother called and asked that she come to Massachusetts. "I need your help, Leah. We need to get your dad into a rest home."

Leah spent the next three weeks in Massachusetts while her three comrades in pioneering set out to find the perfect piece of land in North Carolina. When they all returned to Florida, Leah received the details of their find. The excitement in their voices was evident by the peaks and squeals of their storytelling.

"It's perfect!" Spring Breeze said.

"And blessed by God!" Rock Tree added.

Leah turned to Tim for clarification.

"As soon as we found the land," he began, "a beautiful hawk came swooping down over it."

"Let's do it, then," Leah beamed. "Time to grab our clothes, our animals, and whatever personal items we have left. Time to journey on up to begin life in our own little Utopia."

The moment Leah stepped out of the car in the North Carolina mountains, alarm bells went off inside her head. She pushed them aside, trying to focus on her new home rather than their noisy gongs. But when she saw that in order to reach their land she would have to walk straight up the side of a mountain over a half-mile section of rocks and streams, she realized that there was remote. . .and there was *remote!* And *this* was *remote!*

"For October, it sure is hot," she mumbled to Tim. "And muggy." They made their way up the mountain. "This is so far," she whined.

"I thought you were rugged enough to live like a lumberjack," Tim teased.

"So did I. Now, I'm not so sure. How much farther?"

Tim, Spring Breeze, and Rock Tree came to a stop. "Here we are!"

"Where?" Leah squeaked out.

"Here!" Spring Breeze answered happily.

"We're on the side of a mountain! Where's the level ground? Where do we put our teepees?"

"Oh!" Spring Breeze laughed. "It's over here! Here, you walk this way."

Leah followed Spring Breeze. "Here?"

Spring Breeze nodded.

"Oh, yes! This is beautiful!" Leah turned to say. "I will have to say that this cheers me up considerably! Out of ten acres, we have one beautiful piece of level land. We have lots of trees, streams, and little waterfalls. Where's Tim?"

"Tim went back down. He's going to try to bring the moving van up the side of the mountain to the property."

"What? Is he crazy?"

"Oh, no! He can make it."

Naturally, he could not. Leah lost all semblance of patience. It was late afternoon, the tents weren't up (the teepees had not been purchased yet), she was tired from their trip, and disappointed at most of what she saw. When Tim returned and reported that the van was stuck "but good," Leah's newfound bitterness spewed out of her mouth; her prime target was Tim. When she was done, Tim looked to stand only three inches tall.

"Let's go get the van unstuck," he said softly, turned on his heel, and began to lead the way.

Eventually the van was unstuck, the tents were pitched, and the items necessary for the first night in their new, albeit temporary, homes were brought in. Exhausted, Leah and Tim fell asleep, their last thoughts being that in the morning everything would look better.

They didn't realize that this was only the first night of the hurricane.

"I thought we left hurricane weather when we left Florida," Leah complained to Tim. It was their first night on the mountain, and the tent housing of Spring Breeze and Rock Tree's sons had flooded. They chose to crawl into Tim and Leah's tent rather than their parents'. On the second night, as the hurricane winds continued to blow, Tim and Rock Tree were "on the road" picking up the teepees, while Spring Breeze, the kids, and Leah spent the night trying to keep the fire going and the outside tent (the "kitchen") from blowing over.

"Is it just my imagination, or is the wind blowing stronger?" Leah asked Spring Breeze.

"No, I think it's getting stronger. Much stronger, to be exact."

"Yeah, that's what I was thinking, too." Leah huddled into her jacket and began a fuming process that wasn't going to end anytime soon.

Soon everyone in the little town below knew about the "teepee people," including a sweet elderly couple who had a summerhouse on the mountain, just where the road ended. One afternoon, the couple stopped by the camp. "We've heard about your problems here," they said. "We have a small two-room trailer on our property if you'd care to stay there until this hurricane passes."

"That would be nice; thank you," Tim answered, accepting for the group. And so it was that over the next week four adults, two kids, two cats, and three dogs lived in a two-room trailer. And *not one of them* was very happy.

"But at least we have a bathroom, a shower, and a real stove and sink," Leah noted.

The weather cleared, the older couple made nervous noises about having to leave and close everything up for the season, and the "teepee people" trekked back up the mountain to their property. This time, however, there were teepees to carry. . .in pieces.

"How many teepee poles would you say we have here?" Leah asked, looking down at the poles lying on the ground.

"At least thirty," Spring Breeze answered.

"Uh-huh. And how long would you guess they are?"

"Ahhh, I don't know. . . ." Spring Breeze placed her fisted hands on her hips and looked down at the poles.

"Well, I'm not good at guesstimating, but let me give it a try here. I'd say we're looking at twenty feet in length and oh, I'd say, six to eight inches in diameter."

Spring Breeze rolled her eyes. "Your point?"

"We've got to carry these things. . .all thirty of them. . .up the mountain, over rocks and streams; that's my point! Surely this is a punishment straight from the devil! There's no way you and I can do this alone. We'll have to get one of the kids to help us. If we carry two at a time, that's fifteen trips!"

Spring Breeze sighed. "Let's just get on with it, okay?"

"And," Leah called up to Spring Breeze as they took their first hike at either end of the pole, "has anyone other than me noticed how *hot* it is again?"

"We've got to get these teepees up right away," Tim announced to the group, once everything had been taken to the top of the mountain.

Leah had other things on her mind. *Hmmm, where am I going to put my clothes? Obviously can't keep them in boxes. . .it gets too damp when it rains. Where will I store the cookware? What about food?* she muttered silently to no one. "Hey, everyone!" Leah suddenly volunteered. "Why don't I drive to the nearest department store to buy all the biggest, sturdiest plastic containers I can find?"

"What?" Tim asked incredulously.

Leah pulled Tim aside and spoke out of the corner of her mouth. "I just couldn't imagine even trying to live a day in my teepee without having it organized!"

"Go, then!" he whispered harshly. "But no one here is going to be very happy about you shirking your duty!"

Tim was right. What Leah saw as necessary trips, the others saw as avoidance. The tension among the group began to rise, and most of it pointed toward Leah. This was the beginning of the real trouble, and Leah's personal descent into severe depression.

Leah tried to explain her feelings to Tim, but Tim wasn't listening. "One of the reasons I wanted to participate in this new society was that I *am* different from other people. And I thought that in this Utopian commune, different people would not only be allowed their differences, they would be allowed to use their differences to the good of all!"

"Example?"

"Example? Okay, as an example, I am *not* a morning person. I want to be able to wake up when I wake up, not when the cock crows. In my vision, not-morning-people would do their necessary functions for the community at night!"

"There's not much daylight on the mountain in October and November. Once darkness falls, there isn't anything at all we can do, so for the most part—"

"Okay. You have a point. But it doesn't mean I have to like it when Spring Breeze demands a group meeting at seven o'clock in the morning. Every morning!"

"What do you want me to say, Leah? I don't know what to say to that."

And with that, Tim walked away.

Sleeping in the teepees was nearly impossible. The further along in the season it got, the colder; and the fire only warmed the group if they were sitting directly in front of it. Eventually space heaters were purchased, but it was fairly impossible to heat an area enclosed only by a circle of canvas with a hole at the top. No amount of sleeping bags and blankets made it any warmer. And then there was one other little issue.

"Tim! Do you realize how cold it is in the middle of the night when I have to get up to use the rest room? I'm getting a toilet and putting it in the teepee."

"Oh, no you're not."

"Oh, yes I am!"

Leah headed for town and purchased a port-a-potty, rigged blankets for privacy, and thereby solved her getting-up-in-the-middle-of-the-night problem.

"It's Tuesday again," Leah announced to Tim.

"What does that mean?"

"It means it's going to rain. It rains every blessed Tuesday. And do you see that hole at the top of the teepee?" Leah pointed upward. "Every time it rains, the water pours down the sides of the canvas. Do you know why? Because a teepee is only rain-proof and cold-proof if it's level. We haven't cleared out the area of our property that's level, so—"

"Then let's get that land cleared out and move the teepees."

Leah made a face, but deep down she was relieved. This was her hope all along. This would make the whole thing worthwhile. They chose a little area beside a creek and a little waterfall. In the morning Leah would look outside the teepee door and see the sun rising over the trees, hear the tinkling of the water. It was private, away from the others, and beautiful. Leah knew that once this was done, she could relax and enjoy the rest of the adventure. Then—and only then—could she truly appreciate all the beauty of the land. There, in her own private little area, she could better ignore the fact that the "others" apparently had grown to disapprove of every move she made and every word she spoke. As they remained cheerful and optimistic about everything they were doing, Leah became the scapegoat.

One afternoon as they stood on this portion of the land, deciding which trees should be cut first, their "neighbor" (a sociopath with many guns who lived at the top of the mountain) came by. "What are you doing on Debbie's property?" he asked.

"What?" the four adults sang out together.

Several trips to the realtor and city hall shed light on the truth. They did not own the level ground.

"Would she want to sell?" Tim asked the realtor.

"Yeah, but it's pricey."

The group was basically out of money. The level ground was not going to be purchased.

"I want to leave," Leah said to Tim. "I want to go back to Florida. This is it! The final straw! We have no business here! We have no money. No way to build the communal building. No place to put the teepees. This town pretty much closes up in the winter, so there aren't any jobs! It's cold! It rains every Tuesday! Even the outhouse we rented has been taken back *because it rains every Tuesday;* and the truck can't make it up the mountain to clean it for us, and Tuesday is the day they come to clean!"

"Leah, you gotta have faith!" Tim, Spring Breeze, and Rock Tree exclaimed. "You've gotta have vision; you've gotta stop being the wet blanket!"

Leah turned on her heels and took a hike.

By November, Leah was well on the way to an emotional breakdown. She began to drink heavily and soon was drunk from morning to night. She took on the duty of washing everybody's dishes, and that was pretty much an all-day affair. First she had to heat two big pots of water, and heating them to the right temperature took at least a half hour. Then she would start to wash the dishes in one and rinse them in the other. After a few dishes, the water would cool, the clean water would have soap in it, the soapy water would be filthy black with soot from the fire, and she would have to start all over again.

Then there was the fire. The ever-present fire.

"It's wonderful, having this fire in the middle of our home," Leah remarked to Tim, half-truthfully, half-sarcastically. "A nightmare to keep going, but hey—at least it provides warmth, a way to cook food without going out there with the others. But it also ensures that everything we own is always covered with a layer of wood soot. Do you realize when we go to town to shop, people turn in our direction and say, 'Do you smell fire?' And smoke isn't the only odor that's haunting us. We're not bathing but once every two weeks or so because the creek water is too cold, and we stink!"

Tim smiled, but he didn't say anything.

It was getting close to Thanksgiving, and friends from their hometown of Orlando, Florida (who thought that they were living a marvelous adventure), were coming to spend the holiday with them. Leah was spending all her time in drunken misery. By now Tim had become one of the "others." He wouldn't speak to Leah except to snap. Leah started to muse about how she could get rid of herself, since she was no longer of use to anybody—including herself. She spent two full days thinking of nothing else, but couldn't come up with anything that didn't hurt or might fail and leave her as a vegetable.

Yet, in her thought processes, Leah remembered a time several months ago when Spring Breeze had told her about a program in Orlando called "Getting Well."

"It's geared towards those who were dying of cancer, but since the focus is on living in the moment and finding joy in your own life, it works well on depression also, which is the reason I went. They're very good at providing scholarships for those who have no money. It's run by a group of women, psychologists, who really, truly care!"

Leah called "Getting Well" during her next trip to town.

"I've got friends from Orlando who are coming up here for Thanksgiving," Leah explained. "I can ride back with them if you'll take me."

"Yes, Leah! Come!"

This is my last hope. . . .Leah thought. It was a sobering thought.

Leah knew something was very wrong when it came time to say good-bye to Tim; she got the distinct impression he couldn't wait for her to leave! For the next seven weeks, Leah worked through her alcoholism and depression at Getting Well, all the while assuming she'd return to the mountain when her therapy was complete. That was not to be, however.

Up on the mountain, Tim found himself alone. Spring Breeze and Rock Tree (along with their sons) decided the mountain life was not for them. Tim enjoyed his solitude for awhile, but eventually financial reality forced him back to Florida, where he moved in with his brother. Within a few days, he came to Getting Well and asked Leah for a divorce.

Leah was truly alone. "May I stay an extra week?" she asked the staff at Getting Well. "I'm just not ready to face life. . .I have nothing. . .no stuff. . .no husband. . .no money. . .and no car."

"Of course you can, Leah," she was told. During that week, Leah contacted Sallye in Tennessee.

"Can I rent a space on your couch?" Leah asked like a little girl lost.

Sallye chuckled. "I'm full up with both people and animals, but you're welcome to come!"

"I'm going to spend about a week with Tim's brother, John. He'll bring me up there, but first we need to stop in North Carolina so I can get whatever is left up there that's mine." The sadness in Leah's voice was hard to miss.

While staying with John, Leah spent the majority of the time trying to convince Tim to give them another chance.

"I want out," Tim said firmly. "I'll go with you to the mountain and then to Tennessee, but then I'm gone."

Leah nodded. There seemed to be little hope.

A week later, Leah, Tim, and John headed for North Carolina. When they arrived on the mountain, snow began to fall. . .and fall. . .and fall. They were snowed in for several days—wonderful days—days of relaxation and laughter. But when the snow melted, the trio headed for Tennessee.

For the next two months a loving and accepting "family" again surrounded Leah. Though she had been without money or a car, she felt useful and needed. Her role included housecleaning and dog washing. She kept herself busy. . .and tried to forget Tim.

Phone calls from Tim came fairly regularly; they had to stay in touch because he was paying their mutual bills. But the calls sounded more like business calls tinged with resentment than those of man and wife. As time went on, Leah managed to purchase a car, secure a job, and had her eye on the purchase of a home.

Then, one evening as Leah relaxed with a good movie, the phone rang. It was Tim. "I've changed my mind, Leah. I want this marriage to work. I want you to come home."

A month previous the decision would have been simple: Go home to Tim! But Leah had made peace with Tennessee. She liked her job; she wanted her own place; she. . .she. . .wanted to give her marriage one more chance. "Would you come up here?"

"I've got a good job here, Leah. We'll have to live with John for awhile, but I know we can make this work."

Leah took a deep breath. "Okay, Tim. I'll come back to Orlando."

Living with John and his preteen daughter, Holly, was easy. . .

until the spiritual differences began to surface. John was a devout Christian and Leah was a devout pagan. Shortly after Leah moved into John's home, he disconnected cable to the television.

"Too much violence," he explained.

"Oh! But you'll watch the news. Nothing violent about that," Leah remarked sarcastically. "This is just too much for me! I don't get it! What is going on in my life? I am plagued by Christianity! You play Christian music on the radio. We go out to eat and the next thing I know your church friends are standing there asking if we're all saved!"

The references to Christ came from seemingly nowhere and everywhere at the same time. One night, after watching *Schindler's List*, Leah commented, "He really made a great sacrifice."

"Leah," John began, "let me tell you the greatest sacrifice. . . ."

Leah groaned.

One afternoon, as Leah listened to Jewel's hit record, "Who Can Save Your Soul?" Holly approached her and said, "Aunt Leah, I know who can *really* save your soul."

Leah fumed.

"What's worse," she complained to Tim later, "is that you're buying into all this!"

"Leah. . ."

"Oh, I know! You *used* to be a devout Christian. You went to seminary. But I thought you had gotten past all that! I thought you were as sane as I am! A humanoid God! What a laugh! You are all pushing me as far away from Christianity as I can get!"

Leah began a job that became her "salvation." She worked seven days a week, sometimes sixteen hours a day. Anything to get out of the house where the "goody-goodies" lived. At the end of a year, Leah found she couldn't even speak to her husband or his brother without snapping. Problems mounted with each passing day until finally Tim and Leah realized if their marriage was going to survive, they needed to start over. . .again.

"I'll quit my job," Leah said. "We basically do nothing but smoke pot all day anyway. I've saved enough money for us to move into our own apartment."

Tim agreed, and things were better. . .but not good. Tim was going to church every week. His attitude had truly changed, and Leah saw in him a desire to make the marriage work. She had no such motivation, and his churchgoing was really getting on her nerves. "If you'd stop this nonsense, we'd get a lot further, Tim," she said sarcastically.

Tim took the verbal abuse and continued to attend church. In the evenings, while Leah attempted to begin an Internet business, Tim read his Bible and watched Christian videos on television.

"Watch these with me," Tim would say. Leah loved music, so she'd stop for a few minutes and watch with critical eyes. She didn't want to admit it, but she was forced to be honest. "Hey! Some of this stuff is good!"

Tim smiled. Then Leah added, "Too bad it's all about Jesus!"

Leah had to admit that if Tim was making an effort, the least she could do was have an open mind. She began to ask questions, she tried to read the Bible, and she even volunteered to try church. "But only if we go late," Leah explained to Tim. "That way no one will see me go in. *And* we have to sit in the back of the balcony."

Tim agreed to Leah's conditions, but Leah didn't like church any more the second time she attended than she did the first time.

"Meet with the pastor," Tim encouraged. "Talk to him, Leah. Ask him all your questions."

Leah agreed, but the visit was unsuccessful. Each question Leah threw the pastor's way was answered with Scripture. "You can't convince me the Bible is real by quoting it!" Leah argued. At the end of their time together, Leah mentioned they were living with tight finances while they waited for her business to take off.

The pastor grabbed Leah's hand and began to pray boldly. "Lord, make this business an immediate success!"

Leah went home with hope and a plan. If the business became successful, she might just really look into this Jesus stuff.

The business went down the tubes! Everything she had worked so hard for was. . .gone. Leah went into another depression, spending her days lying on the sofa watching television and complaining to Tim. "I'm not ever going to try anything again. Nothing ever works. I only get my hopes up to get them dashed back down again. I'll just stay on this couch for the rest of my life and hope that I never get stupid enough to try to do anything with my life again. And as for your God. . .well! I took a step and look what happened! He has apparently dropped me down an abyss! This is your loving Jesus?" Leah cursed Him, but later as she stood under the spray of the shower, she began to talk to Him. "If You're even there, You're a *major* disappointment! Obviously, I'm just talking to the shower stall!"

Life's moments became strange. Leah began to feel a yearning inside; she *wanted* Jesus to be real! She *wanted* to give up and give in! Every day she found herself talking to a God she didn't believe was real. After a few weeks, she got off the couch.

"Leah," Tim said one evening, "there's gonna be a Christian concert at a church and I was thinking about going. Would you go with me?"

"What? You're kidding me, right? You want me to sit through Jesus music for hours? Are you out of your mind?"

"Just go to be with me, okay?"

Leah finally consented and the concert moved her. She wanted what the words of the songs talked about. Listening, she thought about a book of Tim's she had been reading, *Left Behind*. She began to think, *You know, if this stuff is true, I'm going to get left behind. Still, I'm too intelligent for this. . . .*

Tim was attending a new church. "Would you try this with me?" he asked. "I understand their music ministry is incredible, and you like music."

Leah had to be honest. "I've heard about their music."

"So will you go?"

Leah sighed. "Yeah. Okay."

The sermon that first service was about having respect for all of God's creations, the animals, the birds, the trees, and the earth. Leah sat up straight and tall in her seat. Finally, someone who saw things the way she saw them!

The following Saturday, Leah asked if they'd be attending the new church again. It was difficult, if not impossible, for Tim to hide his amazement. Something in the services was moving Leah, sometimes to tears, but she was still blasting Jesus in the shower. "This isn't right," she admitted to Tim. "I want to talk to somebody at the church."

Leah called the church, and an appointment was scheduled for her to speak to one of the pastors on staff.

"Not the senior pastor?" she asked.

"No, I'm sorry," she was told. "We'll need to set you up with someone in the Pastoral Care department."

"Forget it. . .well. . .who?"

"We can set a meeting with Pastor Gerald Jones. You'll like him."

"What makes you so sure?"

"Everyone likes him! He rides a Harley!"

Leah's eyebrows shot up. "Really? All right. Let's do it. But you let this guy know ahead of time that I'm not about to sit there and listen to another joker trying to prove a book using the book!"

"I think you'll find Gerald to be very intelligent. You'll enjoy talking to him."

Good, Leah thought. *By the time I'm through with him, he'll* stop *believing!*

On June 9, 1998, Tim took off work to accompany Leah to an appointment with Gerald Jones. Leah was determined to lay some really heavy questions on this guy, but when she did, he answered most of her questions with a perfectly comfortable, "I don't know."

"What do you mean, you don't know? Aren't you going to show me some incomprehensible Bible verse that proves whatever slant you're trying to force?"

"Nope. There are a lot of mysteries. There are things we just don't know."

"Then how do you know it's true?" Leah asked.

Gerald told a story about a rabbi he knew. "The rabbi challenged me intellectually on several matters. I challenged him back. Then I said, 'Open your mind for two weeks. Just believe. After the two weeks, you can go back to not believing. Just have faith, and see what happens.' The rabbi took the challenge. He became a believer."

"Just. . .believe? Without reasons? Without explanations?"

Gerald took Leah's hand. "I can see how badly you want to believe."

Leah began to cry.

"Pray with me," he said softly, then began the Sinner's

Prayer. Leah could hear Tim crying beside her, but it seemed to come from a great distance. The room itself receded as the most calming, peaceful, and yet dynamic energy flowed through her. It filled all the empty places and brought her back to life.

Leah walked out of Pastoral Care in a daze. "What just happened back there?" she asked Tim.

Tim smiled. "Let's go to lunch. How about Friendly's?"

"Yeah. . .okay."

Friendly's overhead music system greeted Tim and Leah when they entered the restaurant, and as they slid into a booth, a new song came on.

"Do you hear that?" Leah exclaimed.

"What?"

"The song! It's Christian! It's Susan Ashton's 'You Move Me'! Friendly's doesn't play Christian music!"

And right then and there, in the middle of a restaurant full of people, Jesus spoke to Leah through the words of a song.

Today Tim and Leah are involved in several ministries, including the Children's Puppet Ministry. They are now a team who works through their problems with commitment. "It was no accident we met," Leah said to Tim one evening after church. "It was the divine hand of God."

And Tim agreed.

Tim and Leah's Precious Verse:

Then they asked him, "What must we do to do the works God requires?" Jesus answered, "The work of God is this: to believe in the one he has sent."   JOHN 6:28–29

To love another person is to help them love God.

SØREN KIERKEGAARD

By faith Abraham, when called to go to a place he would later receive as his inheritance, obeyed and went, even though he did not know where he was going.

HEBREWS 11:8

Genesis Twelve and Twenty-One

Abram and Sarai/Abraham and Sarah

The LORD had said to Abram, "Leave your country, your people and your father's household and go to the land I will show you.

"I will make you into a great nation and I will bless you; I will make your name great, and you will be a blessing. I will bless those who bless you, and whoever curses you I will curse; and all peoples on earth will be blessed through you."

So Abram left, as the LORD had told him; and Lot went with him. Abram was seventy-five years old when he set out from Haran. He took his wife Sarai, his nephew Lot, all the possessions they had accumulated and the people they had acquired in Haran, and they set out for the land of Canaan, and they arrived there.

Abram traveled through the land as far as the site of the great tree of Moreh at Shechem. At that time the Canaanites were in the land. The LORD appeared to Abram and said, "To your offspring I will give this land." So he built an altar there to the LORD, who had appeared to him.

From there he went on toward the hills east of Bethel and pitched his tent, with Bethel on the west and Ai on the east. There he built an altar to the LORD and called on the name of the LORD. Then Abram set out and continued toward the Negev.

Now there was a famine in the land, and Abram went down to Egypt to live there for a while because the famine was severe. As he was about to enter Egypt, he said to his wife Sarai, "I know what a beautiful woman you are. When the Egyptians see you, they will say, 'This is his wife.' Then they will kill me but will let you live. Say you are my sister, so that I will be treated well for your sake and my life will be spared because of you."

When Abram came to Egypt, the Egyptians saw that she was a very beautiful woman. And when Pharaoh's officials saw her, they praised her to Pharaoh, and she was taken into his palace. He treated Abram well for her sake, and Abram acquired sheep and cattle, male and female donkeys, menservants and maidservants, and camels.

But the LORD inflicted serious diseases on Pharaoh and his household because of Abram's wife Sarai. So Pharaoh summoned Abram. "What have you done to me?" he said. "Why didn't you tell me she was your wife? Why did you say, 'She is my sister,' so that I took her to be my wife? Now then, here is your wife. Take her and go!" Then Pharaoh gave orders about Abram to his men, and they sent him on his way, with his wife and everything he had. . . .

Now the LORD was gracious to Sarah as he had said, and the LORD did for Sarah what he had promised. Sarah became pregnant and bore a son to Abraham in his old age, at the very time God had promised him. Abraham gave the name Isaac to the son Sarah bore him.

*By faith Abraham, even though he was past age—
and Sarah herself was barren—was enabled to become a father
because he considered him faithful who had made the promise.
And so from this one man, and he as good as dead,
came descendants as numerous as the stars in the sky
and as countless as the sand on the seashore.*

HEBREWS 11:11–12

To have the rose, you must accept the thorns.

JOE SIN

Mandy's Song

Rick and Pam Bradshaw

Pam Bradshaw had just sat down in her favorite chair after a long day of working at the bank, running errands for her family of four (husband, Rick, and two children: Mandy, nineteen, and Joey, fifteen), and preparing dinner followed by the necessary cleanup. Earlier she had transferred a load of clothes from the washer to the dryer as Mandy ran through the house and out the door leading to the carport.

"Bye, Mom!" she called out in her effervescent way. "I'm going to pick up Erika and then we're going to church!"

Pam looked up briefly. Mandy, a freshman in college who sang mezzo-soprano, was always dashing off somewhere, either to hang out with friends, to a church function, or to Praise and Worship practice. Tonight was no different. "Have fun!" she called back. "And be careful!"

Mandy returned with an obedient "I will!" The door opened and closed, followed by the sound of the family automobile being driven out the driveway.

Now Pam was finally able to sit down and relax, but not for long. The ringing of the telephone brought her out of her chair almost immediately.

"Hello?" she spoke into the phone.

"Hello, Mrs. Bradshaw." The voice belonged to Isaac Hunter, their pastor's son and a longtime friend of Mandy's.

"Hi, Isaac—"

"Mrs. Bradshaw, I just got a call from Erika; Mandy's been in a car accident."

Like most things in Mandy's life, this was nothing new. In nineteen years, Mandy had survived broken bones, concussions, and a couple of fender benders. "Where is she?" Pam inquired.

"They took her to Florida Hospital; the accident was right there in front."

"Okay. I'll tell her father and we'll go up there."

Pam found her husband of twenty-one years outside, enjoying

a late-afternoon cigar. "Rick, Mandy's been in another accident. We need to go up to Florida Hospital."

Because Mandy had driven the family car, Rick and Pam climbed into Mandy's truck and left for the hospital that was only a few miles from their home. As they neared the hospital, Rick slowed the truck down to allow for the backup in traffic.

"Wonder what's going on up there?" he said.

Pam fell silent, a new fear creeping over her. Then she saw it. Pushed off to the side of the road was the car her daughter had been driving—demolished. She screamed and began to cry. From the looks of the automobile, no one could have survived the accident.

Rick, kindled with a father's passion, began to push ahead in traffic. A police officer attempted to stop them from approaching until Pam rolled down her window and yelled, "That's our daughter's car!"

The officer escorted them ahead and within long, agonizing minutes they were running into the emergency center.

"We're Rick and Pam Bradshaw," Rick told the receptionist. "Mandy Bradshaw is our daughter."

Pam noticed the number of paramedics in the area; their eyes focused on them, staring in an eerie silence.

"Your daughter's been airlifted to ORMC," the receptionist said.

Rick and Pam returned to the truck and began to leave the parking area of the hospital. "I'm going to have to stop and get gas," Rick said. "Mandy's always driving on empty."

When they finally arrived at Orlando Regional Medical Center, Rick and Pam were met by friends and fellow church members, Sam and Mary Susan Pratt. Their daughters, Amy and Emily, were best pals to Mandy. Together the four parents walked into the emergency room, where dozens of Mandy's friends had already gathered. Standing in the center of the group was Joel and Becky Hunter, Isaac's parents. Rick and Pam acknowledged everyone as they approached the desk.

"We're Mandy Bradshaw's parents," Rick repeated to the receptionist.

"Have a seat," he was told. "They're working on her now. It'll be awhile."

Everyone gathered together. As the minutes ticked by, other friends and family members joined those already in attendance. Pam's sister, Shannon, and her boyfriend, Justin, a uniformed deputy sheriff, were among those who waited quietly and prayerfully.

"I'm in uniform," Justin said to Shannon. "I'm going back there to see what's going on."

Pam cut her eyes over to where her sister and Justin stood huddled together; Shannon nodded and Justin made his way out of the waiting room, past the doors leading to the examination area. A few minutes later he returned. By this time the hospital chaplain had joined the group.

"It doesn't look good," Justin said quietly, though not quietly enough. Pam took the words in as large tears began to slip down her youthful face once more. Finally, after what seemed to be an eternity, Mandy's doctor came from behind the door barring Rick and Pam from their child. "You can go in," he said. "But only for a few minutes."

Rick, Pam, and Joel quickly followed the doctor. What they saw was stunning. Mandy, just hours before the very essence of life, was lying inert and helpless, countless tubes and wires hooked to her petite body. Joel began to pray; his words came fast and powerfully. Precious minutes later they returned to the waiting crowd that had grown nearly eighty strong.

Sometime later, Rick and Pam were approached by a neurosurgeon, Dr. Ramos. "Can you all follow me?" he asked. Everyone moved forward to a more private room. Fear began to grow inside of Pam. *He's going to tell us our daughter is dead. My. . . how life can change in a second.*

Once everyone was inside the designated room and the door had been shut, the doctor began to speak. "I'm going to be honest with you. This doesn't look good." The sound of sobs began to fill the room. "Mandy's brain stem is bruised. It's the result we see with Shaken Baby Syndrome. Her left arm is shattered, but that's not the main concern. The pressure on Mandy's brain is very high right now, due to the swelling. If it doesn't go down immediately, chances are Mandy won't make it."

"Okay, guys! Let's pray! Let's pray for Mandy!" Joel huddled the group together the moment the doctor left the room. Prayers began to flow from the hearts and lips of those who loved Mandy and believed in God's awesome power of healing. A sweet, calming Presence filled the room. Moments later, the doctor returned.

"The pressure has dropped," he reported. "Drastically dropped! But we still have a way to go."

Rick and Pam looked at each other with tear-filled eyes. *Would their daughter endure this night?*

It was necessary for Rick and Pam to call into work early the next morning and explain their new status. Though thoughts of financial difficulties were nowhere near the forefront of their minds, their lives were about to take on more than just the obvious changes. For three weeks Mandy lingered in intensive care. Three weeks of progressive care followed by three weeks on the floor for neurological care came next. By this time, Rick had returned to work, but Pam's full-time care of their daughter remained necessary. Mandy's life continued to hang on a fragile tightrope; it was imperative that someone be at her side constantly. The bank where Pam worked gave her unlimited time off but without pay.

After the first nine weeks, thirteen additional weeks of hospitalization would follow before Rick and Pam could finally bring their daughter home. Mandy remained in a comatose state; she was totally dependent on her parents, family, and friends for her care and rehabilitation. Pam wouldn't be going back to work anytime soon. The two-income family had become a one-income family with a host of bills. Creditors would have to be juggled. Rick and Pam tore their thoughts from their daughter to focus on how they would meet their obligations. *How were they going to make it through this financially? This could go on indefinitely!* Riveted by faith, they gave their financial problems over to the same One they had given their daughter's physical problems—God.

Their thoughts easily returned to the needs of their child and, as only God can orchestrate, the financial miracles began.

A motorcycle club, whose members included Rick as well as many of his and Pam's friends from church, organized a Motorcycle Ride to benefit Mandy. The Longwood Florida Police Department held a car wash. Mandy's high school drama department gave a two-night performance with all proceeds going to the Bradshaws. Don Sanderson and his orchestra performed at a swing dance, and, remarkably, individuals—some that the Bradshaws had never met or heard of—sent money to aid them in their time of financial crisis. "I know they say that marriages can fall apart after a crisis," Rick whispered to Pam at the end of one of the many emotion-packed days. The room was quiet around them and it felt good to be able to talk intimately about his feelings. "But the more time goes by, I just don't see how. I mean, either you *are* a Christian or you *aren't*. You either believe or you don't."

"It's the foundation our marriage is built on," Pam replied, slipping her small hand into his. "Our marriage is built on godly principles. That's why we can survive this; that's why we can believe."

But sometimes, in the early morning hours when his mind was heavy from sleep, negative thoughts crept in. *Why? How long?* Rick soon learned the only way to win that battle was to replace the questions with prayers.

"God is in control," he and Pam would often say to each other. It became the family's theme.

As the weeks and months become years, Mandy continues to make progress. "We have good days and we have bad days," Pam replied to a friend when asked how things were going. "Some days Rick is up and I am down. Some days it's the other way around. But I never doubted for a minute that we would get through this together. I don't know why this had to happen, but I believe with all my heart that one day Mandy will be back with us as she used to be. . .and we'll hear her sing praises to God once more. Until then, her songs are only for Him. He is as He always was: her only audience."

One evening, tired and weary from another day of physical therapy and medical treatment of her daughter, Pam sat near the hospital bed (now dominating the family living room) where Mandy lay. Rather than retrieving her own Bible from the bedside table, she reached for Mandy's. Opening it, she read Mandy's favorite verse, underlined during better days. " 'For I know the plans I have for you,' declares the Lord, 'plans to prosper you and not to harm you, plans to give you hope and a future' " (Jeremiah 29:11). Pam nodded in agreement. "Amen," she whispered. "Amen."

Rick and Pam's Precious Verse:

His breath is like a rushing torrent, rising up to the neck. He shakes the nations in the sieve of destruction; he places in the jaws of the peoples a bit that leads them astray.

And you will sing as on the night you celebrate a holy festival; your hearts will rejoice as when people go up with flutes to the mountain of the LORD, to the Rock of Israel.

The LORD will cause men to hear his majestic voice and will make them see his arm coming down with raging anger and consuming fire, with cloudburst, thunderstorm and hail.

The voice of the LORD will shatter Assyria; with his scepter he will strike them down.   ISAIAH 30:28–31

Patience with others is Love,
Patience with self is Hope,
Patience with God is Faith.

ADEL BESTAVROS

Two words, friendship and forgiveness. We were friends before we fell in love and we are still best friends (and still in love). Friendship and love are what our life is based on (after Jesus, of course), but forgiveness is what keeps us together after all these years. Of course, we love each other, but it has been my experience that human love is not enough to keep people together. When any two people spend so much time together, one or the other is bound to do or say something that requires forgiveness.

CAROL AND LOYD BOLDMAN,
Married January 25, 1974

*M*ay your fountain be blessed, and may you rejoice in the
wife of your youth.
    A loving doe, a graceful deer—may her breasts satisfy
you always, may you ever be captivated by her love.

PROVERBS 5:18–19

Big Fish, Little Fish

Ted and Elva Weaver

*F*or Ted and Elva Weaver, life in Sweetwater, Texas, was good.
They owned an upscale home with pool, outbuildings, and
apartments, all debt free. Together, they owned a business. Ted
was on the city commission and had a three-year tenure as
Chief Executive Officer of the local Chamber of Commerce. He
worked four days a week teaching at a nearby community college
and was well-known in the community, thanks in part to writing
a weekly newspaper column and hosting his own radio and television programs. Ted and Elva were the "big fish in a little pond."

Life was perfect, or nearly so, until a job with the Texas Edu-
cation Agency was offered to Ted. Taking it seemed the right
thing to do, but it would mean a move to Austin, a much big-
ger pond than Sweetwater. But he and Elva decided it was the
right thing for them and their teenage daughter, Carole.

    The little family moved, and in the beginning all seemed
fine. Then, reality set in.

    "Austin's cost of living is much higher than Sweetwater,"

106

Ted told Elva. "I get paid once a month, and by the middle of the month the money is gone."

"We need to sell the house in Sweetwater," Elva noted.

Ted agreed. "I know. Here we are living in a cramped apartment while in Sweetwater we have an estate-style home sitting vacant!"

Vacant was a word that could be used only from time to time. Frequently, the house and property were victims of trespassers. Adding insult to injury was a sudden hailstorm in Austin that completely destroyed their uninsured automobiles. As if that were not enough, as the family was about to sign a contract on a new home in Austin, the contract was "mysteriously lost."

"I don't mind being a little fish in a big pond," Ted confessed to Elva. "But I do mind being a fish lying on the bank." Ted swallowed hard. "Elva, can I see you and Carole for a moment? Would you get our daughter?"

Within minutes, mother and daughter faced Ted around the kitchen table.

"My paycheck only covers our rent, insurance, and groceries, nothing for clothing, entertainment, or any extras," he began. Elva and Carole stared at him as if they heard the problem but were waiting now for him to provide the answer. Ted's eyes grew wide as he added, "You will both need to get a job, and soon! I'm trying to peddle some used cars on the side and maybe the house in Sweetwater will sell soon. But until then, we're broke!"

Both Elva and Carole jumped to Ted's side and spoke simultaneously.

"Oh, Honey!"

"Oh, Dad!"

"It's okay! We're here as a family!"

"Yeah! Dad, we're in this together! We'll get through this!"

"We love you, Honey! And we're proud of you!"

Elva had always wanted to extend her cosmetology skills into the areas of skin care and color analysis. The situation at hand would lead her to become a *Beauticontrol* consultant. Carole contacted her new friend, Rhonda, a lively redhead who worked as a waitress at a barbecue restaurant. That very week she began a job as a waitress.

Things were remotely better. But the crowning blow came when the estate in Sweetwater sold. . .at less than half the original asking price! The little family held on to each other and to their faith in the Lord. "We have to trust Him now more than ever before," Ted said firmly.

And that they did. It has been almost twenty years since Ted, Elva, and Carole moved to Austin, Texas. While they are still not back to where they were *financially,* they are stronger than ever in their walk with the Lord. In fact, their marriage seemed to actually be strengthened by the difficulties!

Today Carole is married and is a full-time mother to daughters Whitney and Lyndsey. Elva continues to work as a *Beauticontrol* consultant. Ted has done many things, all related to the call of pastoring. He is employed by Motorola and is a community college instructor. Currently he is "on assignment" at a college in Colorado Springs where he teaches Communications and Human Relations.

God continues to meet the needs of Ted and Elva as He uses them to reach others. In spite of the losses, in their hearts they know the truth: They've had a good life.

Ted and Elva's Precious Verse:

"Everyone brings out the choice wine first and then the cheaper wine after the guests have had too much to drink; but you have saved the best till now."　　JOHN 2:10

*One word frees us of all the weight and pain of life:
that word is love.*

SOPHOCLES

The union of husband and wife in heart, body, and
mind is intended by God for their mutual joy; for the
help and comfort given one another in prosperity and
adversity; and when it is God's will, for the procreation
of children and their nurture in the knowledge and love
of the Lord.

Therefore marriage is not to be entered into unad-
visedly or lightly, but reverently, deliberately, and in
accordance with the purposes for which it was instituted
by God.

From "The Celebration and
Blessing of a Marriage,"
The Book of Common Prayer (Episcopal)

After nearly twelve years with the police department, Mike
sustained a knee injury that made it necessary for him to retire
unusually early. He was devastated! I can honestly say he took
the retirement badly! Every day he'd call the station to find out
what was going on, he'd listen to the scanner constantly, and
then call the station to advise where someone was located that
another officer was having difficulty finding. It was two-sided,

though, as some of his coworkers would stop by the house to ask advice on all sorts of matters or the dispatchers would call to ask where something might be located in the station.

Those things didn't really bother me so much as the little things. When we were out in the car, Mike would point to another vehicle and say, "Their inspection sticker is dead." I'd tell him it shouldn't matter to him; he was retired from that line of work now. Or, sometimes he'd say, "I'd write that one up in a heartbeat for reckless driving!" He just couldn't let go!

Finally, I told Mike to turn off the scanner and get on with his life. But my heart was breaking for him because I knew that he had lost one of his dreams. All he'd ever wanted to do was be a police officer right here in his own hometown. So, now, after only twelve years, he finds himself searching for another job, another career, and another direction. I try to tease him by asking him what he wants to be when he grows up.

It's not so much the loss of money as it is the loss of satisfaction; we've never been the glory hounds in the financial realm! But we love life in spite of the hardships. Together, Mike and I teach a Sunday night preteen class at church. Mike is definitely a teacher; he is wonderful with the kids. He becomes very animated in retelling some of the Bible lessons, and the kids become so excited that it's contagious! Personally, I design the summer camp T-shirts, organize fund-raisers, outdoor activities, and holiday gatherings.

I'm very ecologically minded—very aware of the nature that God created for us—and man's never-ending battle to seemingly run it down, so our family has participated in the Ohio River Sweep for many years. This is a multiple-state cleanup effort. Mike, the kids, and I look forward to it every year. . .even if we are picking up trash!

Then, of course, above all else, we have our kids. Donovan

is fourteen, has been dancing for over eight years, and thinks this is what he wants to do professionally. Cassie is twelve and has a beautiful singing voice; she sings at church, at school, and at the Winters' annual family reunion. Krischan is six and is the one who makes me laugh when things in life don't seem so perfect. But, more often than not, he makes me laugh at his antics, so he's easily forgiven.

So, in spite of not knowing what's ahead professionally or financially, we know we are blessed because our lives are full and good. At times Mike becomes overly concerned and worried. Still, God is gracious.

DENEENE WINTERS †

Mike and Deneene's Precious Verse:

He himself gives life and breath to everything, and he satisfies every need there is.   ACTS 17:25 NLT

The real test of friendship is: Can you literally do nothing with the other person? Can you enjoy together those moments of life that are utterly simple? They are the moments people look back on at the end of life and number as their most sacred experiences.

EUGENE KENNEDY

I am my lover's and my lover is mine.

My husband and I have been married since 1974. Our biggest help is that we both try to think of the other as our best friend. I have multiple sclerosis, and the extra trial of this disease has sent many a spouse packing; but my husband says, "It's me and you against the world, and together we can make it through anything."

ELLEN HATCHER,
Married June 21, 1974

There Will Be Peace in the Valley†

Keith and Sarah Patrick*

Keith Patrick was an independent business consultant when he married Sarah. Most, if not all, of his work was with one company, the same company he had been with most of his adult life. As an independent consultant, Keith worked from an office in their California home.

One afternoon, Keith sauntered into the kitchen where Sarah was preparing their dinner. One look at his face told her something was wrong. "What's the matter?" she asked.

Keith sat heavily in one of the chairs flanking their kitchen table. "The company is cutting back the number of hours I can bill per month."

Grabbing a towel and wiping her hands, Sarah joined Keith at the table. "What does that mean?"

"I'm not sure, but it doesn't sound good."

Sarah reached over and patted Keith's hand. She understood his fear—they were newlyweds, but they were not spring chickens—yet she was certain everything would be okay. "Don't worry about it, Keith. God takes care of His children."

Early one morning a few months later, Sarah heard Keith's office phone ring, followed by a monotone conversation. Concerned, she walked into the office. Keith was hunched over his desk, jotting notes on a legal pad, while listening to the caller's voice through the phone he held tightly against his ear. Sarah noted his white knuckles, and she placed a hand tenderly on his shoulder. He didn't even flex or acknowledge her. When the conversation was done, he hung up the phone and turned his face to Sarah. "Six to eight weeks, Sweetheart, and the job is over."

Sarah took in a deep breath. "Are you worried?"

Keith paused as he thought about the question. "No, not really. I'm sure I'll find work with another company. It's just that I've been with this company for so long."

Sarah smiled. "I'm not worried either. We'll be okay."

Keith began to explore other job options, but none of them worked out. "Have you told your kids anything?" Keith asked Sarah one night.

"No, no one. No one in the family knows. What about your children; do they know?"

"No. Let's not say anything yet. I know our kids are grown, but they don't need to add this to their list of things to worry about."

Sarah frowned. "How are we doing financially?"

"Not good, Babe. Nearly three months without steady income has been difficult on our savings account."

Sarah took a deep breath and broached a subject somewhat taboo. "What about the alimony checks to Margaret? Is there any way we can cut that back a little?"

Keith began to shake his head before the question was completely out of Sarah's mouth. "No. I won't cut the amount of the check, Sarah. I owe Margaret that money."

"I agree you owe her alimony, Keith. But do you owe her so much?"

Keith started for the door. "I'm not going to argue with you about this," he said, then left the room, leaving Sarah to stew in her own juices.

Later that day, Sarah received a phone call from her good friend, Jennifer. "Would you and Keith like to come over Friday night for dinner?" she asked.

"I think so. . .I'll check with Keith and see what he says, but I don't see why not!"

"Call me back and let me know," Jennifer said.

Sarah could not have known that this dinner would provide an answer to their flagging finances, but a few nights later, as Sarah and Keith sat across the dining table from Jennifer and her husband Tom, Jennifer said, "Sarah, you should call Janie Patterson!"

"Why's that?"

"You know she's the manager of the ticket office at the Tenth Avenue Christian Center in Garden Grove, right?"

"Yes. . . ."

"Well, they are beginning to gear up for the Christmas pageant—our son has just started doing some data entry for her—and so I was talking to her this afternoon. They need workers because they're changing computer programs. There's lots to be done!"

"Jennifer, I don't know. . . ."

"Oh, posh!" Jennifer exclaimed as she jumped up from the table and went to the phone. Sarah laughed as she heard Jennifer dialing Janie's phone number but sobered as Jennifer explained the situation she and Keith were in. "She can work for you, Janie, and she really needs a job. . . . Sarah, come here; Janie wants to talk with you."

Sarah looked over to Keith and raised her eyebrows. "Oh, well!" she said with a smile. "I don't guess you and I will have the opportunity to talk about this, huh?"

Keith smiled back. This wasn't what he wanted, his wife working—while he combed the want ads of the newspaper—but this did seem to be an opened door and they would be foolish to say no to the money. When Sarah returned to the table, she smiled and said, "She practically hired me on the spot!"

"What did I tell you?" Jennifer grinned from ear to ear. "I should open my own agency!"

Tom shook his head. "Don't even think about it!"

Sarah laughed easily, then looked over to Keith, who forced a smile. She could so easily read his thoughts. He always liked the idea of Sarah being a homemaker, but now was no time for pride. Sarah watched in understanding as he swallowed it along with a spoonful of the dessert Jennifer had served while she was on the phone.

At first, Sarah worked four hours a day, then six, then eight, and toward the end, overtime. When the woman handling group sales left, Janie moved Sarah into that position. In spite of her desire to be at home, Sarah was actually enjoying herself at work. But the income was not nearly enough to support Keith, herself, and his ex-wife; and unfortunately Keith had yet to find a job. With Christmas looming ahead, Sarah wondered how they were going to celebrate the family gift exchange. Then, two weeks before Christmas, Sarah came home to find Keith in a very happy mood.

"I've got good news and I've got bad news," he said.

Sarah beamed at her husband, the love of her life. "From the look on your face, you have good news and you have good news!"

Keith laughed out loud. "Which one do you want first?"

"Um, the bad news!"

Keith shook his head as he took Sarah by the hand and led her to the sofa. "You're getting the good news first!"

"Oh! Okay!"

Together they sat and clasped hands. "The good news is: I got a job!"

"What! Oh, Keith!" Sarah wrapped her arms around her husband. "Just today I was wondering how we were going to make it through Christmas, and God has answered my prayers! Now we don't have to tell the kids what we've been through lately."

"Well, hold up a minute there," Keith interjected. "There's still the bad news."

"What could be bad?"

"The bad news is: We have to move in order for me to take the job."

Sarah's smile quickly faded. "Move?"

"Yeah."

"From our home?"

"Yeah."

"To another town?"

"Yeah."

"Where?"

"Sunnyvale."

"Where's that?"

"Northern California, in the heart of the Silicon Valley."

Sarah took a deep breath and exhaled slowly. "Well, then! I guess I need to call a realtor about selling the house. When do you start the job?"

"January second."

"Whew! It's gonna take a miracle from God to sell the house in that length of time."

"Then we'll pray for a miracle."

A miracle happened. Keith and Sarah's house sold in five days, and the week before Christmas they headed to northern California and the town of Sunnyvale. The excitement at the prospects the new move might shower down on them was quickly squashed when they arrived in town and discovered the only place in the wealthy suburb they could afford was an old trailer in an even older trailer park.

"Nearly a thousand dollars a month for this," Keith said, dejected. "I can't believe I've brought you to this."

Sarah squared her shoulders and made an attempt at sounding hopeful. "No, Keith. This is only temporary. We'll store our possessions in a storage place and begin looking for a proper place to live. We'll be out of here in no time."

This was to be but the first blow for Keith and Sarah.

"Looks like I don't have a job after all," Keith told Sarah.

"What?"

"The man I was talking to had no authority to hire me. I guess I'm pretty naïve, huh?"

"Oh, Keith!"

"I'm sorry."

Sarah didn't know what to say. "It's okay," she muttered, though her words didn't express the sentiment. She silently walked into their tiny bedroom, fell across the bed, and cried.

Keith continued to look for work but with no luck. Money was tight, bills were not being paid, and making alimony payments was a joke. The phone began to ring constantly, and more times than not, it was Margaret.

"I'm doing the best I can," Keith would snap at her. "You can't get blood out of a turnip, Margaret, and right now I'm a turnip. . .yeah, well, do what you have to do!"

Even worse were the times Margaret called when Keith was not at home.

"Let me speak to Keith," Margaret would order.

"He's not here."

"Is that right?" Margaret asked, intimating she didn't quite believe Sarah.

"Yes, that's right. He's not here. I'll tell him you called."

One afternoon Keith came home from his endless job search to find Sarah standing in the kitchen reading a letter. "Whatcha got there?"

Sarah extended the paper. "Your ex-wife's budget," Sarah answered in a huff. "The nerve of that woman. She's driving me nuts! Listen to this: She doesn't understand why this is happening to her. To *her!*"

Keith wadded up the paper and threw it in the trash. "We need to talk about something else."

"What now?"

"We need to take the money from the sale of the house and buy another one pretty quick or we're going to be hit with capital gains taxes."

"I hadn't thought of that. Why don't we go out this week-end and see what we can find?"

The home search became another source of depression. Everything in Sunnyvale was overpriced, old and falling apart, or new and jammed upside the house next to it. The original plan to live in the trailer park for six months was obsolete; Sarah and Keith were now edging close to a year.

In spite of the downside, the strong believers in the power of God found happiness in the little things. Old videos were often checked out from the library. Sarah would pop popcorn and the two of them would snuggle together on the sofa, call-ing it "date night." They went for long walks, and on Sundays they enjoyed a drive and a stop at an ice cream parlor where a cone could be purchased for ninety-nine cents. Sarah and Keith were enjoying life on a very tight budget.

Sarah was learning to be frugal with Keith's unemployment checks. She clipped coupons, watched food ads, shopped at dis-count stores, and sewed her own clothes. More than that, she and Keith determined, come what may, they would not stop tithing. "God stays central in our marriage," Keith said firmly. Sarah agreed completely.

Finally, a job came through for Keith. Eighteen months after their move, having realized that in order to afford a house they would have to move away from the area, they purchased a home sixty-five miles from Sunnyvale. The commute was a bear, but Keith was happy to be employed and—once again—a homeowner.

Years have passed, but the lessons learned during this difficult time have remained powerful in the hearts of Keith and Sarah. "God was faithful," Sarah, who today is a Christian author and speaker, said to one of her audiences. "What amazes me most is

God's sense of humor. Because Keith has so far to travel in his commute, we began to pray that he would be hired by another company, one closer to home. Lo and behold, he was! Three years ago, Keith was hired by a company. . .still in the Silicon Valley. . .and all of a half mile closer to home! Well, isn't that what we prayed for?"

Keith and Sarah's Precious Verse:

And my God will meet all your needs according to his glorious riches in Christ Jesus. PHILIPPIANS 4:19

What greater thing is there for two human souls than to feel that they are joined. . .to strengthen each other. . .to be at one with each other in silent unspeakable memories.

GEORGE ELIOT

This single mother with a high school GED managed to raise four sons by working her way from one position to the next, each time moving into a better-paying job. At one point, I became the "Director of Special Services," for a small credit union. The title sounded much less intimidating than Credit Counselor. My job was to reduce the 22 percent delinquency to less than 5 percent, using the most effective means possible. The project became one of the most rewarding experiences of my career.

Years later, I met Adam. During the first year and a half of our relationship, I learned about his medical bills for an emergency procedure to correct kidney failure and a little about some complications he experienced with his insurance carrier. He told me he closed a checking account shortly after the divorce from his first wife because he was lousy at keeping records. He also told me about the four children from his past marriage and his child support liability. Despite our differing attitudes about economics and financial management, I discovered Adam was an irresistibly compassionate, sensitive, vital, and fun-spirited man. We developed a close, personal relationship that we carefully nurtured as it blossomed into romantic love.

In the eight years since the divorce from his first wife in Los Angeles and his subsequent move to Phoenix, he lived a cash-only existence. He worked in a machine shop days, played in a band three evenings a week, and served as music minister in the church he attended. He was perfectly comfortable cashing his paycheck, dividing the money into envelopes labeled on the outside with the name of the landlord, utilities, the kids, and other commitments, and living on the rest. He knew at some point he would have to put money away for the kids' college expenses and his senior years, but he thought putting the fires out as they popped up was managing well enough for the time. Thinking I'd seen it all, I carefully considered our few differences and determined them to be healthy balancing points rather than potential problems. None of his dark secrets intimidated me— I had already survived raising four adolescent males—I was fearless and ready to take on anything.

Onward we went toward our wedding plans. Little did I know my experiences with my first husband and as a credit counselor/ collections officer scarcely prepared me for the situations that appeared within the first six months of our marriage. Within a week after we announced our engagement, the company Adam worked for announced the facility he worked in would be relocating to California. Those who wished to keep their job could plan to move at their own expense; otherwise severance packages would be negotiated immediately. The decision not to relocate to California was simple for us. However, we decided on moving north to Washington to pursue Adam's vision to build a music ministry within the next year or so. We adapted our plans, postponed our wedding, and made the exodus.

Three months later, we had a private wedding on a Saturday afternoon. I wound up in the hospital on Sunday night with a ruptured tumor that began bleeding internally—a condition I was happily ignorant of until that hour. My second thought as we located the nearest hospital was how we would pay the bills when all I had was my disability insurance. Adam had just started his new job, which didn't offer any benefits at the time. Those concerns quickly gave way to pain. We made it through the terrifying first night and my new husband comforted me, assuring me not to worry, that he and God would take good care of me.

Two months later Adam's words, "Don't worry, Darling, God and I will take good care of you. . ." rang in my ears when I began opening the mail on the way back to the house from the curb, and I saw the red-stamped letters saying, "Past Due—please remit." That night, I learned to my horror that his way of taking care of me was collecting the mail in a box and throwing away the bills because "they always send more copies later on." The notion that a thirty-eight-year-old man in today's society could survive so long with no mind for finance baffled me. For weeks on end, I was on the phone explaining the situation with not only local health care providers, but also the providers of my husband's emergency surgery in Phoenix. I quickly discovered the former employer enrolled Adam in a plan providing dental and life coverage and completely overlooked the basic health coverage he selected first.

Two days and dozens of long-distance phone calls later, the employer agreed to contact the insurance providers and correct the mistake. I agreed to contact all health care providers involved and have them all resubmit their claims, instructing them to refer all further inquiries to the employer's representative by name. That all seemed simple enough—at least it would have been had over eleven months not already lapsed since he generated the initial charges. After so much time, several of the providers were very reluctant to rebill but agreed to try. Three weeks later, I received the first of many notices from collection agencies. The employer's representative failed to mention the company was recently acquired by another company and couldn't find any information regarding my husband's claim. I'd been stalled off until the company no longer existed!

After a quick prayer, sending up a flare for heavenly help, I dialed the number for the corporate office at the new location. As "The number you dialed is no longer in service. . ." faded into a drone, a knock at the door demanded my attention. The postman asked me to sign for two registered letters, one to my husband from a state agency, Department of Child and Family Services, the other from the Internal Revenue Service addressed to my husband and the former wife's name. I set the letters unopened on the desk by the door of our little living area. Knowing why I used registered letters with return receipts when I worked for the credit union, a flood of tears welled up from the depths of my soul. The deluge couldn't catch up with the fear that overtook all reason by the time my husband arrived home. But before he noticed the state I was in, he announced he was going to be laid off from the machine shop where he was working because there would be no more work until late spring. It was December 23.

I entertained thoughts that I'd somehow overlooked my sudden, painless death and gone straight to hell for sin that some demon completely erased from my memory. At one point I remember thinking I could relax because life surely couldn't get any worse. I couldn't imagine then how silly a notion that turned out to be. To feel the freedom the truth enables was hard to recognize those next few months. One of the registered letters announced the nonexistence of a tax filing for the year Adam divorced and the estimated tax, penalties, and interest due, and a demand for back child support from the state where his children reside with their mother. The absence of any receipts for the cash Adam sent to his former wife became a frightening reality when combined with the paperwork he received. It informed him for the first time of a court-ordered payment already $16,000 in arrears. There was also a distinct absence of any mention of what he had already consistently provided.

Somehow we managed through the next few months together—barely. I remember the entire time I worried that perhaps this was my punishment for some covert sin. I spent days wondering if I secretly wanted to be married badly enough that I convinced myself the man I chose was a saint, when all along he was a gigolo and I was the only one who didn't realize it. Only what didn't fit into that scenario was that my life was happy and full when I met Adam. I wasn't looking when we met. During the rare quiet times in my prayer closet, God faithfully reminded me how I had discovered contentment in living alone by simply trusting God. I had (finally) quit my lifelong habit of challenging my heavenly Father over the difficulties I couldn't understand and started obeying Him in every area of my life. I remember my amazement at the many areas I had yet to release to the Lord as He, one by one, revealed them to me.

We knew no one but the landlord and landlady in the small

town that seemed so distant and unfriendly. Daily we wondered how long it would be before everyone in that quaint little hamlet discovered the awful truth that we couldn't pay our bills and we became the source of ridicule at our church. To me, it was a continuous living nightmare—the ultimate irony. Adam's immediately entering a retraining program in our own town seemed like little comfort while I was disabled and unable to work. Daily I cried out to God, working full circle, confessing any sin I could imagine, asking forgiveness for marrying the wrong guy, and pleading for Him to help us honor our commitment to our vows to love, honor, and cherish one another—no matter what.

The concept of pressure took on a whole new personality for us both—this one had hooked barbs. Yet daily the Lord showed us how to soothe and comfort one another despite the fear and doubts that ripped and tore at us both. It wasn't easy to put into practice, but we gradually learned how to express to one another our fears and concerns without attacking or assigning blame. I didn't know until months later, that all the time I worried I had married Casanova in disguise, Adam felt like he had just stepped into the Twilight Zone and rarely managed to stop the terrifying images that came to him in waves. He recently told me that for months during our second year, he dreamed about a neon sign (spelling out the word "loser") flashing over his head all night long while neighbors gathered around outside the window, determined to discover what the peculiar light was all about.

After several months of working with one collection agency and making token payments to as many of the twenty-four health care providers who still worked with us, we were subpoenaed to appear in court to answer for the claims of another of the collection agencies. The judge granted a judgment in favor of the collection agency as though he didn't hear a word we said about our attempts to resolve our debts despite our humble lifestyle. Several counseling agencies advised us to file for relief under the bankruptcy laws, stressing the new reality of garnishment, levies, and other potential hazards if we didn't. Even so, we worked with a Christian credit counseling organization for another year. During that time, we met an attorney through new friends, a dedicated Christian man with an excellent reputation in our community, who helped us come to terms with what seemed like total defeat to us, bankruptcy. The process took another year; but during that time, we learned to run the three-legged race, teaming up together when it seemed hardest to do so, and blocking the fear and humiliation that worked so hard to force us apart.

It doesn't seem fair having to start over with less than nothing, but God meets our every need with amazing timing. We framed the envelopes Adam used to manage his finances before we met as a reminder that God rewards those who diligently seek Him. Even in the trenches, the love we share is beyond everything I ever imagined as an adolescent or an adult on the rebound. God is still able and always faithful. Our cash-only economic policy, rare in today's ever-increasingly cashless society, keeps us certain of God's faithful hand as He leads us onward.

E.V. ALICE LAMBERT

Adam and Alice's Precious Verse:

Now to him who is able to do immeasurably more than all we ask or imagine, according to his power that is at work within us, to him be glory in the church and in Christ Jesus throughout all generations, for ever and ever! Amen.

EPHESIANS 3:20–21

*I have found the paradox that if I love until it hurts,
then there is no hurt, but only more love.*

MOTHER TERESA

*O*ne day I realized that if I am supposed to do everything as unto the Lord, that includes cleaning the toilets!

BECKY HUNTER

I Owe You[†]

Dave and Jane Aldrich

*J*ane Aldrich poked fun at her husband, Dave. "Remember, you still owe me $25,000!"

"Hey, why do you think we stay married?" Dave returned quickly. "I can't afford to pay up!"

Life smiled sweetly on Dave and Jane Aldrich during the first year of their married life. Then, during the second year, a Bible college on the west side of the country accepted Dave. They would leave their home, their family, their friends, and the lives they had known and cherished for so long. Everything would be new and different: the town of Portland, Oregon, their jobs, Dave's school, their church, and, hopefully, their friends. As they crammed all they owned into their car, they gazed at each other

127

with all the hope and love in the world shining in their eyes. Little did they realize the test into which they would be driving.

Their new home had no television—only a radio and a deck of cards. In the first few weeks, while looking for jobs, Dave and Jane entertained themselves with games of gin rummy. Jane kept meticulous records of her wins; Dave would end up "owing" her $25,000.

"I found a job," Jane told Dave one sunny afternoon. "It's close to the apartment, so I can walk and you can use the car for school."

Dave nodded. "We need to figure out the shortcuts to school and church. You up for an outing?"

Jane smiled. "Yes!" She enjoyed going out with Dave. . .no matter the reason.

In no time, Dave and Jane made new friends, but Jane was still lonely for her family. Adding to this was Dave's ministry assignment, which was required by the Bible college. Dave was asked to teach the young people's Sunday school class and direct the choir at the new church they had begun attending. Slowly he and Jane integrated into the church family and had occasional invitations for Saturday night dinners or dessert and coffee after services on Sunday night. These were special blessings in their transition.

Gradually, they settled into a routine and began to feel more comfortable with their surroundings. Then Jane became very sick.

"I think I have the flu," Jane told Dave.

"Are you taking anything for it?" Dave asked.

"Oh, yes. But it doesn't seem to be helping."

Several sick weeks later, Jane went to see a doctor.

"Mrs. Aldrich, you're pregnant," he told her.

Jane stared at the doctor incredulously. "How did that happen?" she asked. "I've been on birth control!"

The doctor smiled and shook his head. Jane frowned, knowing

she would have to tell Dave the news—news that would change their current plans.

Dave dropped out of school and, because he was a trained physician's assistant, he took a job as a night supervisor of emergency at the local hospital.

"The hours aren't great," he commented to Jane. "But at least I have a job."

Dave's new position required him to work nights and nearly all weekends while Jane worked days. As time went on, her loneliness grew. When she gave birth to their son, Jeff, on July 19, 1972, Jane took a six-week leave of absence. But when the time period came to an end, she knew she'd have to return to work.

"Dave, we have a problem." Jane and Dave were driving home from church. "I don't know of a reliable or capable person to baby-sit. I've got to be honest with you; I'm so scared! I wish we were closer to our families or friends back home. These were people we could depend on to help! But out here. . .I don't know anyone— at least not anyone I feel comfortable leaving the baby with."

"We should pray about this, Honey. Seeking God's guidance is the only thing I know to do."

Jane agreed. Still a little frightened, she began to pray for God's provision.

Two weeks before Jane was to return to work, her employer came to visit.

"Jane, I remember my move out here from Tennessee. I remember being far from home, not knowing anyone well, and missing my family. I put myself in your position and wondered if you'd found someone to baby-sit yet?" she asked.

"No, I haven't and I don't want to leave my baby with just anyone. Do you know someone?"

"As a matter of fact, I do. She's a good friend and lives in your area. She has a toddler and looks after infant foster children, too."

The suggestion turned out to be a gold mine! Dave and Jane agreed that God had again been faithful; but while Jane was relieved and grateful, she missed being home with their baby. Weeks turned into months, and Dave and Jane began to feel the strain of work schedules mixed with the adjustment to parenthood. There was one other demand to be reckoned with. Dave's commitment to their church was taking him away from Jane and Jeff.

"Even though I've dropped out of school, I'm still expected to continue in my obligations to the church," he told Jane.

"But, Dave! When are we supposed to *see* each other?"

"I don't know the answer. I only know what I have to do."

The tension on their young marriage deepened, and Dave and Jane became distant. Their loving relationship had become almost mechanical and they were losing each other along the way. In the back of Jane's mind, she knew that things could continue only so long before something had to be done—they would either break up or break down. She shuddered to think they were so close to one or the other.

During this time, Dave and Jane became friends with Olga Stewart, an older lady in their church. Olga and her husband had been pioneer ministers in the Portland area. By the time Dave and Jane met her, she had been widowed for almost thirty years. Olga sensed something special in Dave and Jane, and she often invited them to her home for meals and fellowship. One day, she made a surprise announcement.

"I've decided to attend another church with a friend of mine, so you won't be seeing me on Sundays anymore."

"Oh, no!" Jane exclaimed. "I'm going to miss you!"

Once more, Jane felt cut off and lonely.

About that time, in an effort to cut expenses, Dave and Jane moved to a less expensive apartment. Providentially, the apartment was near the church Olga was now attending.

"Would you like to come to church with me this Sunday?" Olga asked after Dave and Jane had settled in.

"We'd love that!" Jane answered.

The following Sunday, Dave and Jane joined Olga. "I want to introduce you to the pastor," Olga told them as they entered the front doors. "I've known him for many years, and I just know you'll like him!"

Dave and Jane did like the pastor, and even better, they enjoyed the service. Away from the overwhelming demands of their church, they were able to enjoy the atmosphere, soak in the music, truly hear the message, and feel the Spirit of God.

"I've missed that," Dave confided to Jane on the way home.

"Me, too. Dave, we need to talk. . .we need to make some changes."

"I feel the same way. We either make some changes or I don't know what's going to happen. . . ."

Jane turned her head to look out the window. "I know. I feel the same way, too." Her voice was barely audible. "What do you suggest?"

Dave took a deep breath. "Well, for one, I think I need some time away from my duties at the church. My focus—our focus—right now should be each other and trying to bring some restoration back to our marriage."

Jane began to softly cry. She nodded in agreement.

"Let's make each other our first priority," Dave continued. "And God. We need to restore our relationships with God. If we do that, we'll be just fine."

Dave and Jane began to restore their relationship with each other by putting the spontaneity back into their love life. Surprise dates for each other added a new dimension of excitement and anticipation, looking forward to what the other one would come up with. The romance returned.

Dave changed jobs, allowing them more free time to spend together. Over thirty years have gone by. Dave and Jane came to realize that when couples become busy doing "church work," it might gradually become a "chore" instead of "worship and pleasure." As they left the business of doing the Lord's work out of their sense of "have to" and began to enjoy the soaking in of His presence, they drew closer to Him and their relationship with Him was restored. They spent more time in the Word and in prayer. As they grew stronger individually, they grew even stronger as a couple.

This does not mean it was always easy. As the years went by and another child, and eventually grandchildren, were added to their family, Dave and Jane would often find themselves getting too "busy" again. Their loving heavenly Father, however, gently draws them back to His heart and reminds them of His love for them and their love for each other.

"It's time," Jane says to Dave, or vice versa, and the other knows what that means. *It's time for us—a time to refresh our love.*

Dave and Jane's Precious Verse:

"I took you from the ends of the earth, from its farthest corners I called you. I said, 'You are my servant'; I have chosen you and have not rejected you. So do not fear, for I am with you; do not be dismayed, for I am your God. I will strengthen you and help you; I will uphold you with my righteous right hand." ISAIAH 41:9–10

*By wisdom a house is built,
and through understanding it is established.*

PROVERBS 24:3

God is in control. Val and I both know that,
so we don't waste our time and waste our lives
worrying about things—
what if this doesn't happen or this or that.
We just take it as it goes.

CANDACE CAMERON BURE

We have a long-standing, unspoken tradition in
our marriage, and that is neither of us can sit on the
couch if we see the other one working. Now, we've
never said to each other, "Hey! What are you doing
sitting on the couch? I'm over here breaking my back!"
That has never been said. But from the first—even if
I couldn't do what Becky was doing—I wouldn't feel
comfortable sitting there while she was working. And
do you know why? Because that's a form of intimacy.

DR. JOEL HUNTER

*I fell in love with her courage, her sincerity,
and her flaming self-respect, and it's these things
I'd believe in even if the whole world indulged in wild
suspicions that she wasn't all she should be. . . .
I love her and that's the beginning of everything.*

F. Scott Fitzgerald

Marriage Takes Three

Marriage takes three to be complete;
It's not enough for two to meet.
They must be united in love
By love's Creator, God above.
Then their love will be firm and strong;
Able to last when things go wrong,
Because they've felt God's love and know
He's always there, He'll never go.
And they have both loved Him in kind
With all the heart and soul and mind;
And in that love they've found the way
To love each other every day.
A marriage that follows God's plan
Takes more than a woman and man.
It needs a oneness that can be
Only from Christ—
Marriage takes three.

Beth Stuckwisch

In Sickness. . .
and In Health

Be thou magnified, O bridegroom, like Abraham, and blessed Isaac, and increase like Jacob, walking in peace and living in righteousness. . . And thou, O bride, be magnified like Sarah, and rejoice like Rebekah, and increase like Rachel, being glad in thy husbands and keeping the bounds of the law. . .

FROM THE GREEK ORTHODOX MARRIAGE SERVICE

135

I was visiting a church, an old church; the youngest person in the congregation had to be eighty years old. We came to a place in the service where we turned to the back of our hymnals and read responsively. We stood and I noticed the couple sitting in front of me; you could tell they had loved each other for a long, long time. I noticed when he stood that he had thick glasses and big hearing aids in both ears. It took his wife longer to stand because she was crippled in her legs. She had walked in with two canes and her hips bowed arthritically. And then we read Isaiah 35 (NASB). Have you read it lately? It's about when the Lord comes in fullness *that day*. And it says, "They will see the glory of the LORD, the majesty of our God." We're going back and forth between the pastor and the people. And then it came to this part: "The eyes of the blind will be opened, and the ears of the deaf will be unstopped." She reached up and touched his hearing aids; and she just grinned! And the next line is this: "The lame will leap like a deer." He reached down and touched her hip; and he smiled. And I thought, *Oh, God! What a wonderful promise!*

DR. JOEL HUNTER, from his sermon
"Eternity, Healing, and Criticism"

*W*hen you say your vows,
" 'Til death do us part," and you're really faced with it. . .
you know somebody's there for better or for worse.
It's not just a saying.

KIRK FRANKLIN

The longevity of our marriage has been purely God's blessings! Over the years there have been bad times, but it's knowing there will be good times again that helps you to hold on. There are times when you simply have to trust God and the vows you made before Him and your family and friends. Because of that trust, in my mind I can look at the glass and see it as half full rather than half empty. God has truly blessed us with love for each other. It's not the same as it was the day we married; it changes. . .it grows deeper. Since the day we married—no matter what—I've never imagined a day without Tom. If we are in a room full of people, his is still the face I seek in the crowd.

KRIS GRANTZ,
Married August 28, 1971

The hours I spend with you I look upon as sort of a perfumed garden,
a dim twilight, and a fountain singing to it. . .
you and you alone make me feel that I am alive. . . .
Other men it is said have seen angels,
but I have seen thee and thou art enough.

GEORGE MOORE

Couples often recite these wedding vows without giving much thought to the possibility that health issues may arise before old age. Who would have ever thought that before the wedding a strapping young groom would have a lung removed with only a 25

percent chance of survival? I thought about canceling the wedding, but Zed asked me to continue to make the plans. . .that it would give him a reason to live. Two years later, we were anxious to start a family. When it didn't happen right away, we learned something we had not been told before: The surgery he had before the wedding, along with the subsequent treatment, left him unable to produce sperm. We adopted two wonderful children, but shortly afterward I began to notice numbness in various parts of my body. Three years later, I was diagnosed with multiple sclerosis, resulting in resigning from my career but beginning my own company. At one time I had nurtured my husband-to-be. Now he nurtures me. There have been times when I have not been able to walk, and he carried me up and down the steps. If I could not lift my leg to get in the tub, he would put me in and bathe me. He always remains positive and uplifts my spirits. When he sees that I am overdoing something, he makes me aware of the possible consequences. He goes with me to the doctor. He focuses on the positive things about me and things I can do rather than what I cannot do. My husband does or has taught himself how to do just about everything in the house. He cleans, washes clothes, folds clothes, and more. Anything that I am unable or don't have the energy to do, he does willingly. He even tried to learn how to comb my daughter's hair, but we had to draw the line at that task. Through it all, God has blessed us in so many ways!

RHONDA OWEN-SMITH

Zed and Rhonda's Precious Verse:

When you pass through the waters, I will be with you; and when you pass through the rivers, they will not sweep over you. When you walk through the fire, you will not be burned; the flames will not set you ablaze.   ISAIAH 43:2

*A good marriage is that in which
each appoints the other guardian of his solitude.*

RAINER MARIA RILKE

Problems

Take Them To
The Lord
In Prayer
You Will Find
Your Solution
There.
And Never
With The Answer,
Go Ahead
Until
"Proceed"
He Has Said.

HELEN GARRETT

When Beth Said, "Pray!"

Gerald and Beth Martin

There were nearly forty-eight hours between the time gymnastics coach Gerald Martin met fellow coach Beth Divens at an annual competition in Michigan and the moment they decided to marry. They never actually dated. In fact, Gerald was in a committed relationship with a young woman named Becky.

"If you call my house and Becky answers," Gerald instructed Beth, "don't use your real name. Before we can move forward with our relationship, I need to break things off with Becky."

A life filled with deception began. When Beth called Gerald and Becky answered, she identified herself as Kaci. It didn't take long for Becky to sense that Beth was a presence to be reckoned with. When she approached Gerald with her suspicions, Gerald used the opportunity to sever their relationship.

He then placed a phone call to Beth. "Look, Beth, I'm moving from Ohio back to Texas. I've decided not to train for the '88 Olympics like I thought I would. I can get another job as a stockbroker in Austin and put some distance between me and Becky. There's another thing. . .something I need to talk to you about. . .I'm addicted to cocaine. Do you still love me?"

Beth knew very little about drugs and certainly nothing about addictions. "Will you be able to quit doing drugs?"

"Oh, yeah! With the move, I'll get straight."

"Then, yes. I still love you."

Gerald moved to Houston, but Becky soon followed him. Weeks later, Beth flew down to Texas to end her strange courtship with Gerald. But a few days later the two of them returned together to Beth's hometown in Michigan. "If we're getting married, we're doing it now!" Gerald said.

Blindly, Beth agreed. She knew Gerald had problems, but she loved him and was quite certain her love for him would cure all that ailed him. *Things will be fine,* she told herself. They would rent an apartment in the complex where she had previously lived. She would continue to work as a gymnastics coach and Gerald would secure a job at a local brokerage firm.

From the get-go, Gerald rewarded every emotion with a joint of marijuana. If he was happy, he smoked; if he was depressed, he smoked. If things went well at work, he smoked; if the market was down, he smoked. Beth, who was shy and had never made friends easily, was concerned, but became even more so when her ever-popular husband became friendly with a couple of maintenance workers from the complex. One night the four of them ended up at a crack house together where there were balancing scales for weighing drugs sitting on the kitchen table. Beth immediately knew she wanted nothing more to do with them. Nor did she want Gerald to continue in the relationship. But she found she had little say in the matter.

Then "Black Friday" struck the stock market. Depressed, Gerald took off for a friend's house in Kentucky. Unbeknownst to Beth, he had gone there to commit suicide.

"This is not a marriage!" she told Gerald over the phone. "This is not at all what I had in mind!"

Gerald agreed, but when he returned, he faced Beth with a new revelation. "I'm going to admit myself into a rehab center," he said. "And then when I get out, I'm going to divorce you."

And with that, he left.

Beth dropped to her knees on the floor. "Oh, God!" she cried out. "You've got to help me!"

Though Beth had been raised in a Christian home, she had not been living a life of service to God. Yet God heard her plea for help and blanketed her with a sense of wisdom and peace unlike anything she had ever felt before.

Over the next several weeks, Beth attended family days at the center and the meetings held for spouses, family members, and friends. She called Gerald often, pledging her loyalty to a man she wasn't sure would stay with her once he was clean and sober, but she didn't tell her family the truth about what was happening in her life.

Then, on Christmas Day 1987, Gerald was given a four-hour leave. During that time, in order to continue in their charade, they visited Beth's family for the holiday celebration. The short visit was enough to convince Gerald that he was now okay. He released himself from the program and came home to Beth.

"Beth, while I was in the program I started reading the Bible, and I'm thinking we need to start going to church."

Beth smiled. "While you were gone I started praying and seeking God. I think we should go to church, too!"

Truly united for the first time in their relationship, they began to attend Beth's parents' church and sought counseling from one of the pastors.

Then, unexpectedly, one evening as Beth was beginning the last hour of coaching one of her classes, she received a phone call. Leaving her students, she answered the phone in the office. "Hello?"

"Beth?" Beth could hear a cacophony rising above Gerald's voice on the other end of the line.

"Gerald? Where are you?"

"I'm at the airport. I'm boarding a plane in two minutes."

"What?"

"I'm going back to Texas. . .back to Becky. I've taken half the money, and your car is parked at the Holiday Inn next to the airport. You'll need to get your girlfriend to drive you to pick it up. Good-bye, Beth."

The phone slipped from Beth's grasp as huge gasps began to convulse her body. She knew she had students waiting for her just beyond the door, but she couldn't stop the torrent of tears. This year had been too much for her. A wild thought ran through her mind: *Next week is the annual meet where Gerald and I met.*

Beth immediately went to see the pastor who had been counseling them.

"Don't contact him, Beth. Don't call him and don't write him. Don't allow him to return to you until he breaks all ties with this woman."

Beth agreed. Before she went home, she stopped by a local bookstore and purchased *Tough Love* by Dr. James Dobson. After reading it from cover to cover, she decided the only way she could deal with Gerald was by applying the principles outlined in the book. Still, on occasion, she would call him; but as soon as he picked up the phone, she would hang up. She just wanted to hear his voice.

Shortly after leaving, Gerald called Beth on a Sunday afternoon. "I want a divorce," he told her.

"I won't give you one. When I married you it was for life."

"Then I'll get an annulment!" he said defiantly.

"Gerald, you're not Catholic and we weren't married in the church. Besides, this marriage has been consummated."

Gerald voiced his anger, but Beth managed to stay calm. "Look, Gerald. You do what you have to do. I'll be here waiting for you."

The following week, Beth attended a gymnastics meet in Alabama. When she returned, she learned that Gerald had frantically been trying to contact her, but no one had told him where

Beth had been. As soon as she settled in from her trip, she called Gerald.

"Beth, I want to come back home. I've made a mistake."

Beth's heart leapt, but she remained steadfast in her resolution. "Gerald, before I'll let you come back, there are some things you'll need to do. . . ."

Gerald returned in February 1988. Over the remainder of the year, life was good. Gerald did well as a stockbroker. Beth continued to work as a coach. Then, in December, Gerald's brother announced he'd need to live with them for awhile. Just knowing he was coming triggered something dark inside of Gerald. The afternoon of his brother's arrival, Gerald went out to purchase marijuana. He wasn't able to find anyone with any to sell, but he was able to find someone selling "crack" cocaine. This was a new drug for Gerald, and while Beth entertained her brother-in-law, Gerald was out all night. In reality, Beth was alone.

By May 1989, Beth was pregnant, and Gerald once again cried out for help. "I know of this rehab center," he told her. "It's really nice. It's for professionals like me. They play golf there, eat nice meals. I want to go there and get some help, Beth. It's five thousand dollars, though, and I don't know if we can afford it."

Beth knew where her husband's words were heading. She had received an inheritance from her grandparents, enough money to cover the expense of the fancy rehab center. Beth consented and—once again—Gerald entered a program.

"Beth, I want you to meet someone," her mother told her. "His name is Al Bufkin. He's the director of Prison Fellowship in Detroit. I think he could be a real asset to you and Gerald."

Beth met Al and later introduced him to Gerald. The two men became fast friends. Gerald did well under the program, was released, and, jobless, returned to live with Beth. As he looked for work, Beth continued to coach, but her due date was fast approaching.

"Gerald, I'm not going to be able to work for awhile after the baby comes. You need to find a job."

The request was all Gerald needed to hear to feel boxed in and pressured. Two weeks before their daughter Meagan was born, Gerald began to use crack cocaine again. It was now September 1989, just two and a half years since Gerald and Beth first met.

The night before Thanksgiving, Gerald pulled an all-nighter. At six o'clock Thanksgiving morning, the phone next to Al Bufkin's bed rang. "Hello?"

"Al? Al, this is Gerald! I need help, man! I don't want to be like this. . .I don't want to be doing this anymore!"

Al sighed deeply. "Gerald, why don't you and Beth and the baby come to our house for Thanksgiving? Just come. We'll talk this out then."

That afternoon, after the meal had been eaten, Al handed Gerald a photo album. Flipping the pages and pointing to the various photos of himself, he said, "You see this? This is me when I wasn't doing drugs. And this? This is me when I was." Gerald looked at the photograph of the man who only faintly resembled his friend. "And this is me after God set me free from drugs."

Gerald couldn't believe what he was seeing. "I can't imagine you on drugs," he said. "I mean, I can only see you in the role you're in right now." For the first time, Gerald had a clear understanding that he could truly get better.

A month later, as Christmas approached, Gerald was still jobless. He remembered a friend in Texas who had offered him a job coaching gymnastics should he ever need it. Gerald placed a phone call and was anxious to give Beth the good news!

"I got a job, Beth! I called a friend of mine back in Texas. He'll hire me as a coach for his gym."

"Texas? Why leave here and go to Texas?"

"It's a good job, Beth. It's not a lot of money, but it's something."

"How much money?"

"Twenty thousand a year."

"Twenty thousand? Gerald, I make twenty-five thousand a year and I'm only part-time. Why would we move from our home to make five thousand dollars less?"

Gerald shook his head. "It's a chance to start over. I'm going."

Gerald moved to Austin and, a few months later, Beth and their daughter loyally joined him. They became involved in a church and made good friends with the worship leader, Rick, and his wife, Stephanie. But it didn't take Gerald long to find trouble. By May 1990, Gerald was again jobless and addicted. One night when Gerald didn't come home, Beth called Rick.

"I've had it," she sobbed. "I don't know what to do!"

"Do you want to leave him?" Rick asked.

"I don't see any other way. I'm going back to Michigan, but I don't want to leave my stuff here. He'll only pawn it for drug money."

Rick paused for a moment before answering. "I've got a shed on my property. I can get a friend of mine to help load your stuff up and bring it over here. Do you have enough money for a plane ticket?"

Beth answered between sniffles. "Meagan has a little pink chair with a place where I can hide money. I've got enough put away for a ticket."

"Okay. We'll be over in a little bit."

Beth called her mother next. "Mom, can I come home?"

Beth's mother didn't hesitate. "Yes, but we're changing our phone number and you will not give it to him. If he needs to contact you, he can do it by mail."

Beth agreed. By noon the next day, she and Meagan were settling in at Beth's childhood home. Gerald still didn't even know she was gone.

When Gerald finally arrived home, Rick was there to meet him. "Where are they?" he demanded.

"She's gone, Gerald. She took the baby and she left. She's not going to be here to enable you anymore."

Gerald was angry for awhile but soon saw this as an opportunity for him to break free of his obligations. He continued to depend on Rick and Stephanie until one day, aggravated with the whole thing, Rick exclaimed, "I'm done here, Gerald! I'm through helping you! I'm going to give you over to the devil!"

"Could you put some peanut butter and jelly sandwiches on the porch before you do? I'm starving!"

Back in Michigan, Beth and her family would gather once a week to pray specifically for Gerald. In July, she returned to Austin for a week to allow him to see their daughter. Gerald, now working as a phone book deliveryman and spending most of his time in crack houses, looked awful; he was no more than 125 pounds. Still, Beth resolved not to return, for doing so would only enable him to get worse.

Shortly after Beth and Meagan returned to Michigan, Gerald landed a job with a top computer company. "This is it," he told himself. "I'm going to get clean and do well in this job. First, I'll have one more night on the town before I begin my job in the morning."

That night, in the drug slums of Austin, Gerald was brutally beaten. It wasn't the first time he'd been faced with death during a drug buy. This time, however, the dealers had mistaken him for an undercover officer. And this time, he had a job to go to the next day.

The lies mounted as the using continued. Gerald was habitually late, or "sick," or so tired he slept under the break tables during lunch. It was now September 1990.

Back in Michigan, as Beth's faith continued to grow, she felt an urging from God to begin to pray in specifics for Gerald and to have others do the same. She made a list of people she felt God was directing her to open up to; half were in Texas and the other half were in Michigan. Every two weeks, just before Gerald would get his paycheck, she wrote letters requesting specific prayer needs for her husband. Near the first of October, she attended church with her sister. The pastor talked about "ragamuffin people," people who are often times given up on by man before God is truly through bringing them to Him. Beth knew she was on the right course and that she simply had to hold on.

One afternoon, she received a call from Rick's wife, Stephanie. "Beth, Gerald looks so bad! It's really gotten worse. He's incoherent. He can't stay in a conversation but for a matter of minutes."

Beth didn't allow the words to pierce her heart and shatter her belief that God would be faithful. Instead she continued to pray, not allowing her faith to waver for the husband she loved with all her heart.

On October 30, 1990, Gerald received another paycheck. For the next two days he binged. On Monday, November 1, as he was attempting to get ready for work, he cut himself shaving.

"Ouch!" he exclaimed, looking at his reflection in the

bathroom mirror. What he saw shocked him. Staring back was a skeleton of a man with blood pouring down one side of his face. He picked up the phone and called Rick.

"I think someone gave me some bad drugs. I'm bleeding all over the place and I'm really sick."

Rick was firm. "Here's what I want you to do. Go to work. Tell your employers the truth. Be honest with them, Gerald. We'll be here praying that they'll send you to get some help."

Gerald followed his friend's advice. That very morning, Gerald's supervisor, Jack, took him to a nearby outpatient drug rehab center. Later that day, Jack called Beth and told her that Gerald would be in the program as he continued to work for the company. As soon as she could, Beth called her husband. Stephanie was right; he was incoherent.

Two weeks later, Beth and Meagan returned to Texas to be with Gerald. When she saw him for the first time, she was appalled. But she was home. Together with the Lord, she and Gerald would make this marriage work.

Though Beth had forgiven Gerald and returned to him, it took a long time for her to get over the bitterness she felt in her heart. She had become calloused and wanted to punish Gerald for what he had done. When she spoke to him, it was biting. She didn't want him to touch their daughter; she wouldn't allow him to touch her. *Not until he's perfect,* she told herself.

Finally, Gerald approached her with his frustration. "You need to see what I have done, not what I haven't done yet!"

Beth stopped breathing for a moment. He was right! "Oh, God! Help me again!" she called out. "Help me to stop feeling bitter against the man I love."

God was faithful. Her heart was released from the negative emotions plaguing it. She and Gerald became one again. They became active in church and, for the first time, they began to tithe, even on their small income! A few months later, their faith was tested when everyone in Gerald's department at Dell was promoted but him. He came home that night, depressed and sullen. But he came home. For the first time in their marriage, Gerald didn't face a trial with drugs. Two months later, he received a promotion that escalated him over all those who had previously been promoted.

Nearly thirteen years have passed since Gerald and Beth made a vow to love, honor, and cherish each other for as long as they live. Today Gerald is a successful businessman who lectures at banquets, seminars, and church services about winning the battle over addiction and becoming financially independent. Beth, now the mother of three daughters, continues to coach gymnastics and homeschool her children. Together, they spend countless hours counseling others walking down the rocky road they've long since left behind, and they never miss an opportunity to aid those who are in financial dire straits. It's the least they can do; it's what was done for them.

The gift continues.

Gerald and Beth's Precious Verse:

And we know that in all things God works for the good of those who love him, who have been called according to his purpose. For those God foreknew he also predestined to be conformed to the likeness of his Son, that he might be the firstborn among many brothers. ROMANS 8:28–29

To fall in love is easy,
even to remain in it is not difficult;
our human loneliness is cause enough.
But it is a hard quest worth making to find a comrade
through whose steady presence one becomes
steadily the person one desires to be.

ANNA LOUISE STRONG

Marriage is a. . .lot of hard work!

MARIA SHRIVER

Fred and I have learned along the way that we are very different. Not only our personalities, but our food tastes, sports interests, even the books we read. What has helped us is the realization that marriage is not two people on a bicycle built for two, but rather it is two people riding their own bikes and choosing to go in the same direction. Sometimes one may fall behind and then get a surge of energy and pass the one in front. Sometimes we may ride side by side, but always we know the other is on the same path, heading for the same destination. We have learned to enjoy and appreciate the other's interests and in so doing have expanded our own horizons to make new and exciting discoveries. We are two independent people who have chosen to blend our unique lives into one strong bond held together with a commitment to each other and the Lord.

BETTY SOUTHARD (Author of
The Grandmother Book, Thomas Nelson),
Married January 31, 1957

∞

The courses of true love never did run smooth.

WILLIAM SHAKESPEARE

∞

Coping with Celiac

Don and Sheila Haines

Sheila Haines bent her arm, bringing her elbow into her view. She studied the rash that had formed an itchy patch there, then began to scratch it. "I think I may have picked up something while working in the garden," she commented to her husband, Don, a nurse.

Don peered at the spot his wife was indicating. "You'd better get that looked at, Honey."

"Should I call our GP?"

Don shook his head. "No, why don't you go ahead and call a dermatologist? You'll get a better answer that way, I'd think."

A few days later, Sheila came home from the dermatologist's office with a bottle of pills in her hand. She extended the bottle to her husband and frowned. "He says I might have to take these the rest of my life."

Don was instantly concerned. He turned the bottle so he could read the label. "Dapsone."

"Do you know what it is?" Sheila asked.

"No, but I'll look it up in the *PDR*. Did he tell you what the problem might be?" As a nurse, Don knew that "might have to take these the rest of my life," meant "chronic illness." As a husband, he didn't like what he was hearing.

"No, but he collected some fluid from the rash and said he'd have to have some test run on it. Then he said if it's what he thinks it is, this medicine would help."

Don nodded. "I'm going to look this up in the *PDR*."

The *PDR (Physician's Desk Reference)* is a sort of bible for medical personnel. Within the thousands of pages, one can find nearly everything one would want to know on drug information, diseases, contraindications, and so forth. Don wanted only to find out about one: Dapsone.

According to the *PDR*, the primary uses for the drug were leprosy (which he knew Sheila didn't have) and something called *dermatitis herpetiformis*. Don's brow furrowed. This was a new term for him, and he became even more concerned when he read that Dapsone was not a drug to be taken lightly. Don reached for *The Merck Manual*, the most commonly used medical text in the world.

As he studied the pages describing *dermatitis herpetiformis,* Sheila walked up behind him. "What does it say?"

Don was cautious, not wanting to place unnecessary fear in his wife. "Dapsone is used for a condition called *dermatitis herpetiformis.*"

"What's that?"

"According to *The Merck Manual*. . .let me read this to you. . . 'a chronic eruption, characterized by clusters of intensely pruitic vesicles, papules, and urticaria like lesions.' "

Alarm rose in Sheila's voice. "*What* does *that* mean?"

Don chuckled. "In layman's terms, it means you have a fluid-filled rash that itches like crazy!"

Sheila turned on her heel. "I didn't need a book to tell me that!" she laughed.

Don took a deep breath and exhaled, then looked back to the book. According to the manual, a strict gluten-free diet would alleviate the symptoms. *The dermatologist said nothing about diet,* Don concluded, *so the medicine must be enough. . . .*

Years later, Sheila began to complain of joint pain, particularly in her elbows. Early one morning she sat on the edge of the bed and rubbed the tender area. "Do you think I'm getting arthritis?" she asked Don.

Don laughed. "We're not getting any younger, Honey!"

Sheila smiled back at her husband; but after awhile, as the pain intensified, Don decided she should go to the doctor for a uric acid level, the test used for determining arthritis.

Sheila's test came back normal.

Shortly thereafter, Sheila began to complain of intestinal symptoms, cramping, and diarrhea. She wasn't one to complain; Don was rightly concerned.

Heavenly Father, he prayed, *I've loved Sheila for over forty years. Up until now we've had a good, healthy life. To me, she's as pretty today as she was when I first met her at seventeen. But now she's sick and we need to get her some help. I know at some point all couples will come to a time when one or the other can no longer go on. Is this happening to us now? So soon?*

Don took Sheila to a physician at their local hospital. "I can't explain the joint pain, Mrs. Haines, but I feel the digestive symptoms are due to one of the more common digestive problems.

I want to run some tests, not only to rule out the common problems, but also to rule out something more serious. You've experienced a significant weight loss, so I think this is the best way to go."

When Don and Sheila returned from the hospital, Don could tell Sheila was not 100 percent comfortable with the avenue the doctor was taking.

Don wrapped his bride in his arms. "Neither am I, Honey. But we have to do something. We're caught in the middle of a situation that can't wait. In the meantime, I'm going to call Dr. Stephen James."

"Who's he?"

"He's a gastroenterologist. Better yet, he's a clinician and a researcher. I got to know him when I was working at the Center for Vaccine Development at the University of Maryland."

"Okay," Sheila replied weakly.

When Sheila and Don went to see Dr. James, she quickly recounted her symptoms.

"Sheila, what's your ancestry?"

Sheila and Don looked at each other in surprise. "I beg your pardon?" Sheila asked.

"Your ancestry? Would you happen to be Scotch-Irish?"

"Yes, I am!"

"Uh-huh, I thought so. It looks to me like you have celiac disease."

"What's that?" Don asked, shifting to the edge of his seat.

"It's a chronic intestinal disorder caused by an intolerance to gluten. The symptoms are bone pain, weight loss, abdominal discomfort, diarrhea, and skin disorder."

Don and Sheila looked at each other again. "Oh, my goodness," Sheila said meekly. "Years ago I had this rash. . ."

Don frowned. "When Sheila had the rash, I read about

adhering to a gluten-free diet, but I thought with the medication. . .I feel so badly. . .I. . .I wonder why the dermatologist didn't say anything about her diet!"

Dr. James shook his head in understanding. "Don't beat yourself up over this, Don. Most patients with *dermatitis herpetiformis* seldom advance to celiac disease. And he probably didn't understand the connection between the illnesses and your wife's ancestry."

"What is the connection?" Sheila asked.

"Medical science doesn't really know the answer to that. It just seems to be more prevalent in those of Scotch-Irish descent."

"What measures do you suggest we take, Dr. James?" Don asked.

"A strict gluten-free diet."

"What will that mean?" Sheila asked.

Don chuckled. "My nephew has the best line about a gluten-free diet." Don turned to Dr. James. "My nephew is a physician in Massachusetts," he said by way of explanation. "He says, 'You take everything off the shelf and eat what's left.' "

Everyone laughed easily, but things would seriously change for Don and Sheila Haines.

Don and Sheila like to eat out about once a week, but for Sheila this can prove hazardous. An innocent-looking salad can have a smidgen of gluten-containing substance in it, leaving Sheila very ill. A trip to a pizza parlor means Sheila packs her own rice cakes. When the pie arrives at the table, she scrapes off the topping, transfers it to her rice cakes, and has her own version of pizza. And pasta? Pasta is out.

"Don, you like Italian. Let's go to an Italian restaurant tonight."

"There's little to nothing there you can eat, Honey."

"I'll find something on the menu."

"But I'm willing to give up Italian food! As far as I'm concerned, it's a small price to pay for you."

"Yes, but I'm not willing for you to pay that price."

Sheila and Don are retired now. In spite of celiac disease, they enjoy an active life. They travel easily, namely because Sheila has spent time educating herself about her disease. She's learned what she can and cannot eat and that when she is tired, she must rest.

Recently Sheila forgot her diet. During a family cookout, with children and grandchildren surrounding them, Sheila was having such a good time, she inadvertently picked up a cheeseburger and took a bite. The next day she paid the price.

"That's okay," Sheila said. "This time I don't mind! After all, aren't our grandchildren supposed to make us forget our problems?"

For more information about Celiac Disease: Celiac Sprue Association/United States of America, Inc., P.O. Box 31700, Omaha, Nebraska, 68131-0700, (402) 558-0600

Don and Sheila's Precious Verse:

"My command is this: Love each other as I have loved you."
JOHN 15:12

The way to love anything is to realize that it might be lost.

G. K. CHESTERTON

Oh, what good will writing do?
I want to put my hand out and touch you.
I want to do for you and care for you.
I want to be there when you're sick
and when you're lonesome.

EDITH WHARTON

It was an exciting weekend, January 1998. I had been looking forward to that trip to Los Angeles for months. Since my husband, Joe, and I had moved to the Phoenix, Arizona area several years ago, I rarely went back to L.A. Joe's career in film production keeps him there a great deal of the time, and he flies home on weekends. After eighteen years of riots, fires, floods, and earthquakes—I decided to opt for a calmer, less volatile locale.

The reason for this particular trip was to attend the wedding of one of my very dearest friends, Gayle. I remember how beautiful she looked as she walked down the aisle as one of my bridesmaids. We had been through just about everything together over the years—troubles and happiness.

For Joe and me, life was good. I had just completed the manuscript of my first novel, *Web of Intrigue,* for a successful Christian publishing house, Joe was working on the crew of a very successful NBC television show, and we had just moved into our first brand-new home.

From our hotel window, I could see the studio location below. The January weather in L.A. was, as usual, rainy and dreary. But my spirits were so high. I was excited to be there again. Even with all the things I really disliked about this town, it does have an energy that just cannot be captured anywhere else—especially if you are part of the film community.

Sometime between Thanksgiving and Christmas, I had noticed a lump on Joe's neck. Our family doctor felt it was a swollen gland but wanted him to see a specialist. I had finally urged him to make the appointment. That morning, Joe had an appointment to see an ENT (ear, nose, and throat) specialist.

I was busily trying on the beautiful dress I had just purchased for the wedding, when the phone rang. Joe was supposed to call to let me know what time to meet him for dinner on location.

I answered it with a happy, "Hi, Honey!" But it wasn't Joe. I was startled to hear an unexpected voice. It was Dr. Line, the ENT. Years before, he had treated me for a nagging sinus problem and had remained as one of my doctors. There had been no question that when Joe needed to make this appointment, he would see Dr. Line. We both knew he was the best.

But there was something wrong. Dr. Line's familiar voice sounded strange. Not the casual, friendly, "Hello," I was used to hearing. Without ceremony, he said words that I could not grasp.

"Misty, Joe has cancer. And it's a bad one." The unbelievable words ripped at my heart.

"Nooooo!" I screamed. "You're not calling me. You must be calling someone else. Please be calling someone else."

I was on the floor, on my knees, grabbing at furniture, screaming and crying into the phone. "No. Please tell me it's not true. Please! Oh, it can't be true. My Joe doesn't have cancer. He doesn't!" The pain I felt was worse than anything I had ever experienced.

But nothing I said was going to change the facts. And, the next day, while cameras took beautiful pictures at Gayle's wedding, a sterile CAT scan crawled across Joe's body recording ugly, frightening images of the enemy that threatened to take his life.

Again, St. Joseph Hospital was thrust into my life. The tests confirmed our worst fears. It was tongue and neck cancer. Stage four. A fifty-fifty chance was all he had.

I was so angry with God. How could He allow this to happen to Joe? Joe was such a good and decent man. And he loved God.

While this was a devastating surprise to us, it was no surprise to our God. For the first time in my life, in the midst of this horror, I truly "felt" God's presence. He was there with us. I had no doubt. Throughout the coming months, as He opened my eyes, I began to see with total clarity. Coincidence had played no part in what was happening to Joe and to me. God's hand was no longer invisible—I could trace it clearly.

Why was I in Los Angeles to be with Joe on this very weekend? I rarely went there. It had been months since my last visit. Why did we already have a relationship with one of the top ENT doctors in the country—whose specialty was *exactly* the cancer Joe had?

"For this purpose I came to this hour," God whispered. "I will never leave you."

We had Los Angeles Christian friends who came to be with us at the hotel that very night. We prayed together. Why was Joe so at peace and completely sure he would beat this? Why had I just completed a novel, only days earlier, that I would not possibly have been able to work on during the coming months?

This was no coincidence. God's hand was moving mightily. My God knew what was coming and He had provided exactly what we needed—putting it all in place years, months, and days in advance. He was in complete control.

I admit my fears were not only for my husband. I feared I

would not be able to be the caregiver I knew he was going to need in the coming months. Was I going to crumble? I not only begged for Joe's life, but for the strength I could only have if God gave it to me.

As the months passed, I realized I was doing all the things I thought would be impossible for me. I learned to give the medical attention and IV feedings. God kept me alert and able. It was a true miracle. There were so many times when things were so overwhelming that I felt like I wanted to run. To hide. I didn't want to be going through this—but there was no choice but to go on.

Even though I was angry *at Him,* God never let me down. Never turned from me. When I needed extra strength, it was there. When I felt I could not go on. . .I did. . .and I did it all because of and through His strength. My anger began to subside as I gave up trying to control the storm surrounding us. He was faithful. His promises were true. God was in control.

On April 11, 1999, we celebrated our twelfth wedding anniversary. Only weeks after this anniversary, God bestowed the most wonderful gift on us. We received word that my beloved husband and best friend had valiantly come through months of chemotherapy and radiation to defeat cancer!

All glory and thanks be to our God! He stood with us. Held us when we cried and lifted us when we thought we could not go on. Our Lord continues to be our strength and our hope as we go into each new day.

SUSAN MISTY TAGGART

Joe and Susan's Precious Verse:

But the LORD is with me like a mighty warrior; so my persecutors will stumble and not prevail. They will fail and be thoroughly disgraced; their dishonor will never be forgotten.　　　　　　　　　　　JEREMIAH 20:11

*L*ove does not consist in gazing at each other,
but in looking outward together in the same direction.

ANTOINE DE SAINT-EXUPÉRY

Because He Belongs to Me

Tony and Ann Addison

Tony and Ann Addison had been married thirty years when Tony retired. Over the next four years, he enjoyed his new freedom; then in 1992 Tony awoke in the middle of the night with abdominal pain.

"What's wrong?" Ann asked; Tony's movements in bed had awakened her.

"My stomach's hurting, right here," Tony said, indicating the affected area.

"Are you going to be sick?"

"No, I don't think so. I'll be all right."

The next night, when the symptoms reappeared, Ann got up and called "Ask a Nurse."

"You need to take your husband to the nearest emergency room," the nurse on the other end of the line suggested.

A blood test at the hospital revealed something abnormal

within the pancreas. "You need to see your doctor," the emergency room physician said. "Demand that he do an ultrasound. Demand it."

On Monday, Ann and Tony followed the order. The doctor there thought Tony needed an upper GI first. "No," Tony insisted. "I want an ultrasound done first."

The ultrasound was performed, followed by an immediate call to the doctor, suggesting a CAT scan.

"I want to see you and Ann in my office tomorrow," the doctor said over the telephone.

"Something's wrong," Tony said softly to Ann, revealing fear in a way that only a whisper can.

"Large cell diffuse lymphoma," the doctor said the following day. Tony and Ann listened intently as the doctor continued. "You have a growth on the stem of the pancreas. Because of where it's located, it's inoperable, I'm sorry to say. We'll start chemo as soon as possible."

Tony and Ann had no idea how their lives were about to change. Ann quit her job as a schoolteacher so that she could help take care of Tony as he underwent chemotherapy. Over time, the chemotherapy lowered his immune system, resulting in two bouts of *Pneumocystis pneumonia* (commonly seen in AIDS patients). Chemotherapy was stopped for a period of time in an effort to build Tony's immune system up.

Bringing Tony home from the hospital meant Ann had to learn how to do the IV therapy. A home health nurse came to their home and patiently taught Ann how to administer drug therapy.

"Ann, we can't find anyone to take your place as the high school chemistry teacher. We hate to ask this. . .we know you're going through a lot. . . ."

Ann sighed deeply. "I can come back part-time," she said.

For the next two years, Ann got up early to give Tony his six o'clock medications, went to school, and returned home in time to give the eleven o'clock dose. The third dose was given at four in the afternoon and the last one at nine o'clock at night.

Further complications arose when the chemotherapy damaged Tony's heart muscle, resulting in cardiomyopathy. Ann's once-active husband could do little more than sit in a chair and watch television. For Ann, one of the most difficult things was dealing with Tony's anger and frustrations, especially when Ann hired someone to paint their house.

"The housepainter didn't scrape the windows in the front bedroom," Tony said to Ann one day after the painter had left.

"Tony. . ."

"He didn't! And he left the ladder where I don't like it left."

This time, Ann ignored him, an ability she wasn't always able to keep. When the yard needed maintaining, Ann hired six men, all of whom Tony listed complaints against. "They didn't edge the yard like I like it," he said.

"What's wrong with it?" Ann asked.

"It's too close to the edge."

"The last guy edged too deep. The guy before that didn't cut the grass the correct height."

All this was truly petty in March 1998, when Tony was admitted to the hospital in Columbia, South Carolina. A new IV therapy was started; but by the end of the month, it was obvious that he could not live without the drugs, therefore, weaning him was impossible. On March 24, Tony was transported by ambulance to the University of South Carolina in Charleston. Ann followed in her car.

While Tony was at the hospital in Columbia, he had developed a painful staph infection in one of his eyes, resulting in a near loss of the eye. Antibiotic eyedrops were administered every half hour around the clock; the regimen continued in Charleston, as well. The infection eventually was gone, but the eye would not heal.

"It's called a corneal abrasion," the doctor told Tony and Ann. "We're going to sew his eye partially shut to keep it from getting infected again."

Meanwhile, Tony needed a new heart, and getting one was more complicated than he and Ann could have ever known. First, measurements had to be taken of the heart to give doctors hard data that a transplant was actually necessary. Then both Tony and Ann had to undergo psychiatric evaluations.

"I guess they want to make sure we aren't kooks!" Ann teased.

A dermatologist was called in to check Tony for skin cancer. CAT scans were made of everything that could be made; an MRI of the brain, ultrasounds, ultrasounds, ultrasounds! Tony was tested for TB, double-checked to assure that his cancer was, in fact, gone, and tested to assure sufficient lung capacity.

As Tony and Ann waited for the transplant, they continued to visit the eye doctor in Charleston. On Thursday, May 14, 1998, the eye doctor dropped another bomb.

"The eye is getting worse," he said. "I want you to see a specialist."

The following day, Tony and Ann listened to the choices the specialist gave. "We can sew the eye completely shut. This means you will have no vision in that eye. Or we can try to bring up part of the white of the eye to cover the abrasion so it's not exposed. If it's not exposed, it won't get infected."

"Let's do that," Ann and Tony agreed. "Let's try to cover the white of the eye."

"You won't be able to see as well out of the eye," the doctor advised. "But it will look normal."

"Let's do it," Tony said.

The surgery was scheduled for three days later, May 18, 1998.

The following day, May 16, Tony received the call he had been waiting for. "We have a heart, Tony. You'll need to come to Charleston tonight. We'll do surgery in the morning."

Ann called their pastor, who was camping at a local lake with his family, then packed their bags and the two headed for Charleston. They arrived around nine o'clock that night and their pastor arrived shortly thereafter.

As Tony was being prepared for surgery, Ann rested in the peace that only comes from God. Nearly two months previous, as Tony was being evaluated, Ann read her Bible.

"Ninety-one." God impressed the number on Ann.

A nurse that Ann knew to be a Christian walked into the room. "God keeps giving me the number ninety-one. What do you think that means?"

"Just listen to God," the nurse assured Ann. "He'll tell you."

God did just that; Ann turned to Psalm 91.

From that moment on, Ann was not afraid. Tony's upcoming surgery was no exception; Ann was confident in God's abilities.

As Tony was wheeled toward surgery the following day, he and Ann encountered Tony's eye surgeon.

"I can't have the eye surgery in the morning," Tony told him. "I'm having a heart transplant today."

"I'll talk to your cardiac surgeon to inform him how to keep the eye protected during the surgery."

Tony's surgery began around ten o'clock Sunday morning.

While their pastor stayed with Ann in the waiting room, their church's substitute preacher turned the eleven o'clock service into a prayer service for Tony. Ann and Tony's son, who lived in Charlotte, arrived midmorning to wait with his mother, who quietly prayed as she sat thinking, *This all seems so unreal.* Yet, at the same time, she was bathed in peace. By six o'clock that evening, the surgery was over. Tony had a new heart.

A week later, Tony's eye healed.

Tony was released from the hospital in late June 1998, just in time to celebrate the fortieth anniversary of his marriage to Ann. Their son took them out to dinner.

Today Tony is back to doing the physical chores around his and Ann's home. As Ann watches her husband moving about the yard, taking care of whatever needs to be done, she offers up a song of praise.

Tony and Ann's Precious Verse:

PSALM 91

He who dwells in the shelter of the Most High
will rest in the shadow of the Almighty.
I will say of the LORD, "He is my refuge and my fortress,
my God, in whom I trust."
Surely he will save you from the fowler's snare
and from the deadly pestilence.
He will cover you with his feathers,
and under his wings you will find refuge;
his faithfulness will be your shield and rampart.
You will not fear the terror of night,
nor the arrow that flies by day,

nor the pestilence that stalks in the darkness,
nor the plague that destroys at midday.
A thousand may fall at your side,
ten thousand at your right hand,
but it will not come near you.
You will only observe with your eyes
and see the punishment of the wicked.
If you make the Most High your dwelling—
even the LORD, who is my refuge—
then no harm will befall you,
no disaster will come near your tent.
For he will command his angels concerning you
to guard you in all your ways;
they will lift you up in their hands,
so that you will not strike your foot against a stone.
You will tread upon the lion and the cobra;
you will trample the great lion and the serpent.
"Because he loves me," says the LORD, "I will rescue him;
I will protect him, for he acknowledges my name.
He will call upon me, and I will answer him;
I will be with him in trouble,
I will deliver him and honor him.
With long life will I satisfy him and show him my salvation."

*Your life and my life flow into each other
as wave flows into wave,
and unless there is peace and joy and freedom for you,
there can be no real peace or joy or freedom for me.
To see reality—not as we expect it to be but as it is—
is to see that unless we live for each other
and in and through each other,
we do not really live very satisfactorily;
that there can really be life only where there really is,
in just this sense, love.*

FREDERICK BUECHNER
The Magnificent Defeat

My husband and I struggled, but the one thing we never did was complain. Though we didn't have much to start with, we always gave thanks for what we had. We were a happy family and laughed and played and cried together. I am a firm believer in tithing and praise God for how He prospered us and gave us a beautiful home and four lovely, healthy children who all have done very well. We had ups and downs, but we never carried grudges. We would have our fights and then get over it. We passed this down to our children, who today love the Lord and are practicing the same in their marriages. You have to be big enough to say "I am sorry" when you are wrong, and big enough to accept an apology and then to forget what happened. This is my belief.

GLORIA CARAPIET, Married May 13, 1948;
temporarily separated by death on July 7, 1993

*Love alone is capable of uniting living beings
in such a way as to complete and fulfill them,
for it alone takes them and joins them
by what is deepest in themselves.*

PIERRE TEILHARD DE CHARDIN

Vacuum

Ken and Suzy Ryan

Suzy Ryan stared in disbelief as the vacuum she was pushing whirred, coughed, sputtered, and died. The silence that followed was deafening; all Suzy could do was gaze at the old machine with sad eyes. Years ago she had bought this vacuum from her favorite door-to-door salesman, her seventeen-year-old brother, Bart.

"I know we can hardly afford it," Suzy told her new husband, Ken. "But no one else in the family is going to buy one, so I did."

Ken agreed; money was tight. But he also agreed to the purchase because he knew the special bond between Suzy and Bart.

Suzy and Bart had different fathers and their mother had married numerous times, so their loyalty to one another remained a security over the years. Bart was bright, witty, and had a tender spirit, but he never had any friends. He always seemed content to follow in Suzy's shadow, and she was happy to have him as a close part of her life. When Suzy was old enough to date, Bart accompanied her. He attended football games for the sole purpose of watching her cheer on the sidelines. He kept special gold medals she earned running track. During the summer months, while Suzy sat in the lifeguard chair at the town pool, Bart sat at its base and sipped on her Coke. Bart trailed, and Suzy loved every moment of it!

"He's always filled a void all my achievements could not," Suzy told Ken one evening as they discussed the connection she and Bart felt. "But at eighteen, when I left for college, I felt as if I'd abandoned my own son. I remember driving away from the house for the first time. I glanced in my rearview mirror and there was Bart, peddling his bike as fast as his eleven-year-old legs could go. You should have heard him, Ken. He was yelling, 'Hurry home, Suz! I'm going to miss you!' It took everything I had not to turn around and take him with me."

"Then what happened?" Ken asked, shifting slightly to look at his new bride.

"Then Mom remarried again and left the state, so I didn't see much of Bart during the next few years. . .those precious, tender years when he was in high school. That's why it's so important to me that our relationship rekindle."

A few months later, Bart received his GED and landed a job selling vacuum cleaners. During the week, he lived with his mother, but on weekends he drove seven hours to Ken and Suzy's condo and spent the three days with them. It was during one of those visits that Suzy purchased the vacuum now lying dormant on her floor.

She dropped to her knees beside it and began to examine it for any signs of life. Flipping it upside down, she remembered the phone call from Bart a few weeks after the purchase.

"Hey, Suz! My car broke down. Can you come pick me up?"

"Where are you?"

"Not far," he answered, then gave the directions.

"I didn't even know you were in town!"

"I've only been here for a little while."

"I'll be there shortly and I know of a mechanic we can call. They'll tow the car and look at it for you."

When Suzy picked Bart up, she became immediately concerned. Not only had he kept his arrival in town a secret, but he also looked distant and edgy. A few hours later, after receiving a phone call from the mechanic, Bart flew into a rage.

"Bart, what is it? What's wrong?"

"Can you believe this? Two days to fix my car!"

Suzy spread her arms wide. "You can stay here! We'll have fun!"

"That's not it! That's not it at all!"

For the next few hours, Bart paced in frustration. When Ken came home, Suzy pulled him aside and whispered her fears. "Mom told me recently she thinks Bart may be into drugs."

"What do you think?"

"I don't know what to think. What should I do?"

"I think you should talk to him, Suz."

Suzy sat Bart down shortly afterward. "Bart, I want you to know I love you and I'm here for you."

Bart crinkled his nose. "You know Mom and her exaggerations. She isn't telling me what to do and it's making her mad. I'm fine. Believe me?"

"I can't deny Mom loves to control her children," Suzy laughed. "Okay, then. I believe you."

But the next day, when Bart drove off, Suzy had a fleeting thought. *I'll never see him again.*

For the next two days, Suzy prayed silently for the brother she hadn't heard from since his departure from her condo. "God, make him call! You are sovereign! Please give me one more chance to talk to him!"

He never called, but their stepfather did. "Suzy, Bart committed suicide. They found him in his car. . .carbon monoxide. . ."

Suzy dropped the phone and began to scream, wailing from somewhere deep down inside of her. "Nooooooooooooooooooo! Nooooooooooooooooooo!"

For forty-five minutes, Suzy's lament continued. Finally, when neighbors knocked on the door and inquired about the noise, Suzy calmed, but only on the outside.

That evening, when Ken came home from work, Suzy clung to him helplessly. "Could I have prevented him from doing this?" she cried. "Oh, Ken! Today's his eighteenth birthday! How could this have happened? What if I had found a psychiatrist? Insisted on therapy with him? He had tried this once before. . .when he was fifteen. . .but he wouldn't talk about it later! What could I have done, Ken? Tell me!"

"You couldn't have done anything, Suz," Ken soothed. "Bart was manic depressive. . .he took medication but wasn't faithful with it. You couldn't have done anything."

Over the next several months, Suzy swam in a sea of depression. Her new husband attempted to be supportive, but in reality he expected her to be fine sooner than she was. "You need to snap out of this, Suz."

"How can you be so unfeeling?" she cried.

"I'm not being unfeeling, but I just don't know what to do to help you!"

"Then don't do anything. . .just leave me alone!"

"I can't leave you alone, Suz. I'm your husband. . .at night when we're in bed, I'm aware of the nightmares you're having."

Suzy quieted. It was true. During the day while at work, she was able to hold on to some semblance of normalcy. But at night, the nightmares were the only relief from insomnia.

Suzy's marriage was suffering and so was her home. For the first time in her highly organized life, she was too tired to return a phone call, clean her house, or even wash her hair. Ken, family, and friends stood by helplessly as the raft she clung to lost a little more air each and every day.

Suzy's aunt finally gave her a phone call. "Suzy, may I suggest something?"

"I guess so."

"Have you ever heard of BSF?"

"I don't think so." Suzy sighed deeply.

"BSF is a national nondenominational group called Bible Study Fellowship. It's very intense and I think you'd like it."

Desperate for help and always in pursuit of knowledge, Suzy agreed to attend. "Why not?" she answered.

At BSF, Suzy's world began to spin in a new orbit as she learned to apply Scripture to real-life situations. When she read the words of Jesus in Mark 14:8 ("She did what she could"), she heard the sweet voice of her Savior whisper to her heart. *"Sweet Suzy, you did what you could. I know how much you loved your brother. You couldn't do any more. You did what you could."*

Suzy's tears began to flow freely, but these were new tears, different tears than before. These tears were cleansing. Her life and her marriage to Ken began to heal. "I've neglected you," she told him later. "I'm so sorry. Please forgive me."

Ken wrapped his wife in his arms. "You know I do."

Their marriage flourished and they decided to start their family, beginning with a son, Keegan. Twenty-one months later, Lauren followed, and then their youngest son, Trent, completed the family a year and a half after that. Suzy was truly happy, but Bart's death caused her to ponder things differently within the lives of her children.

One evening, when Keegan was crying because Suzy wasn't going to be able to join his class on a field trip, she felt distress creep into her heart. She looked to her husband and said, "I know I have to teach Keegan that I can't always be available, but it feels like I'm cutting off my arm when I disappoint him!"

"You mustn't allow yourself to feel that way," Ken replied, though he knew what Suzy was truly thinking. *Would disappointment in her lead to depression within Keegan?*

"I can't help it. This morning Keegan threw a tantrum on the way to school. I tried to discipline him, but I ended up screaming instead, which led to tears. Mine and Keegan's. I worry that if I'm a bad mother—"

"You're not a bad mother, Suzy."

Suzy paused for a moment before adding, "Did I tell you what Lauren said to me the other night?"

"No."

"You know how I always find an excuse to return to their rooms after I tuck them in?"

"Four or five times? Yeah."

"On the fifth time of peeking into Lauren's room, she says, 'Mom, I am almost asleep. Could you not come back in and talk to me anymore?' I had to laugh!" Ken chuckled, too.

Then Suzy sobered. "Mom says that Keegan has Bart's personality."

"Suzy, you are not powerless when Keegan disobeys."

Suzy nodded. "I know. After the incident this morning, I was talking to God. I said, 'God, he is not Bart, and even though he has the same sensitive spirit, he won't kill himself.' I know I'll never understand Bart's life or why he felt the need to end it. When I get to heaven, I'll have the answers," Suzy reassured herself.

It was a good thought. . .until the vacuum cleaner broke and

Suzy began to cry. Realizing that it was old and unable to be fixed, she pulled the plug from the wall outlet and sadly shook her head. Somehow she had deluded herself into thinking it symbolized her love for Bart. If it died, she had erroneously rationalized, then her love for him would die as well. Now she knew better. "It's time to part with you, old pal," she said sadly to the vacuum.

The next afternoon, with her three children in tow, Suzy went shopping for a new vacuum. As the salesman showed her the latest in sweepers, she thought of the worn appliance she had thrown away that morning. "I'm ready to let go of the accountability for my brother," she had said to her husband. "I'm ready to concentrate on God's gifts. Bart's death nearly destroyed our marriage and it nearly destroyed me, but I believe what the Word says in Joel 2:25. 'I will repay you for the years the locusts have eaten. . . .' The vacuum in my life caused by Bart's death is being replaced by the peace of Christ. I'm finally free."

Ken and Suzy's Precious Verse:

Do you not know? Have you not heard? The LORD is the everlasting God, the Creator of the ends of the earth. He will not grow tired or weary, and his understanding no one can fathom. He gives strength to the weary and increases the power of the weak. Even youths grow tired and weary, and young men stumble and fall; but those who hope in the LORD will renew their strength. They will soar on wings like eagles; they will run and not grow weary, they will walk and not be faint.   ISAIAH 40:28–31

Ask any parent if they would take on their child's illness, and without blinking an eye they'll answer, "Yes!" There's a helplessness involved in watching any loved one who is ill, but that emotion is compounded by a sense of anger when it's your child. Something rises up inside of you and screams, *I'm this child's parent! I should be able to do something!* Too often, the inability to heal results in an impulse to lash out at one's spouse; they become easy targets. But that gets you nowhere and only adds another chink in the armor. The only *real* thing to do is pray, together and apart. Pray and believe.

EVA MARIE EVERSON

Sparrow Watching†

Jimmy and Lucy McGuire

The shrill of the phone ringing jarred Jimmy and Lucy McGuire awake. As Jimmy answered the phone, Lucy glanced at the digital clock on the bedside table. It was one o'clock in the morning.

"Hello?. . .Hello? . . .What?" Jimmy pulled the phone away from his ear and looked at it in puzzlement.

"What is it?" Lucy asked groggily.

"I don't know. A Hispanic operator said, 'Lucy McGuire. Lucy McGuire.' Then, 'Paul McGuire.' And then she hung up."

Lucy bolted upright at the words. "Jimmy, call Paul's apartment in Buenos Aires!"

As Lucy waited, she began to shake. Their son, Paul, was six thousand miles away, working in Argentina as an English teacher. What could be happening to her baby?

"Juan," Jimmy said anxiously, "this is Jimmy McGuire. Is Paul there?"

"No, he's not," the roommate answered. "I'm expecting him tomorrow."

Jimmy hung up the phone and turned to Lucy. "He's not there. Juan says he'll be home tomorrow."

Lucy's head fell back to the softness of her pillow. "Heavenly Father, please supply his every need. Put a hedge of protection around him. Surround him with your guardian angels." She then turned to Jimmy and spoke into the stillness of the night. "The last time I talked to Paul," she said, "he mentioned that he felt as if he had the flu, but was getting over it. He mentioned the 'grippe' again."

When Paul was a child, his pediatrician explained to Lucy that Paul was "allergic to weather changes."

"We call it *grippe*," the doctor had said. "It's a malaise that people in big cities get."

"What causes it?" Lucy had asked.

"Weather changes combined with pollution. The symptoms are similar to a cold or the flu."

Now, lying in bed beside her, Jimmy confirmed what his heart hoped was true. "I'm sure that's all it is, then."

The next morning, another call came. Again Jimmy answered the phone. When he replaced the receiver, he turned to Lucy in puzzlement. "It was Buenos Aires again. I don't know who called, but he said that Paul was in emergency surgery."

Lucy's eyes grew wide. "For what?"

"Acute something. I couldn't understand him, Lucy, but I

think he was saying something about Paul's appendix."

Lucy began to cry. Her shoulders drooped and her head hung low. "I've got to go there! I want to be with my son!"

Jimmy walked over to where Lucy was standing. Wrapping her in his arms, he began to comfort her. "I know. Let's pray, Lucy. It's all we can do for now."

Jimmy and Lucy knelt at the foot of their bed and began to pray. "Father," Jimmy begged, "guide the surgeon's hands. You love Paul more than we ever could. You formed him before he was even born. Father of all life, please be with him and touch him with Your merciful, healing hands. Please, please heal him."

When they had finished praying and had dried their eyes, Jimmy attempted to phone their friend, Reverend Marcelo Robles, the pastor who had invited Paul to Buenos Aires. When he didn't answer, Jimmy began to place calls to other pastors they knew in Argentina. As he continued in his task, Lucy used their second phone line (recently installed for a home-based business) to get on the Internet. Frantically, she typed out a prayer request to both foreign and domestic prayer warriors. From where she sat, she could hear Jimmy as he continued to phone Argentine acquaintances from their bedroom.

Moments later, Lucy signed off-line, then called their other sons, Jeremy and Jonathan. "Pray, boys," she said. "Pray for Paul."

"We will, Mama," they assured her. "We'll pray right now."

Lucy held the phone in her hands for a few minutes after completing the calls. "What are you doing?" Jimmy asked from behind her.

Turning, she answered. "I don't know whether to call my mother or not. She's eighty-six, and I don't know what this might do to her. Then again, a grandmother's prayers are powerful!"

"I think you should call," Jimmy said.

The call was made.

"Lucy," her mother said after hearing what Lucy had to report, "call the American embassy."

"Mom, I had forgotten about the possibility of them being able to help us!"

"Call your state representatives in Washington. They can give you the number."

When Lucy hung up, she turned to Paul and relayed her mother's idea. Jimmy immediately called Washington, got the number to the American embassy, and then called Argentina. When he hung up, he said, "The embassy is sending someone over to the hospital."

Later in the day, the phone rang. As Jimmy took the call, Lucy stood close by and listened to her husband's side of the conversation. When Jimmy hung up, he turned to Lucy. "It was the embassy. They've requested our son be moved to a private room. Paul's appendix has ruptured, infection resulted, and the surgery was successful; but they say we need to get him out of the hospital as soon as possible." Jimmy finished relating the news to Lucy, buried his face in his hands, and sobbed in relief. Lucy stepped into her husband's arms and began to weep with him.

The phone rang beside them. When Jimmy answered, it was two of the Argentine pastors with whom they had left messages.

"We've seen Paul. He's in terrible pain and in a terrible hospital. Please, let me urge you to have him moved!"

"The American embassy said the same thing," Jimmy said.

As soon as Jimmy hung up, he began to dial a list of numbers the pastors had given to him. Finally, he looked at Lucy in exhaustion. "They say they can't move him as long as he's in this condition." Jimmy's voice trailed into weary silence as the phone rang again. This time, it was Marcelo.

"I have an English-speaking doctor here," he said. "Let me put him on the line."

Jimmy looked at Lucy and mouthed: "It's Marcelo." Lucy dashed into another room and picked up the extension.

"Marcelo?" she said anxiously.

The tone of Marcelo's voice changed from serious to compassionate. "Oh, Lucy."

Lucy placed her hand over her rapidly beating heart, knowing that Marcelo understood how they felt as Paul's parents.

"Don't worry," he said. "We are taking good care of him."

"Thank you, Marcelo!"

"Don't come to Argentina, Lucy. There is nothing you can do here."

Lucy nodded as tears spilled down her cheeks. Words were not necessary, nor would they come.

Hours later, the telephone rang again. This time, when Lucy answered, the weak voice of her son whispered, "Mama, don't come. You couldn't stand to see this place."

"Paul, are you all right?"

"Marcelo is here; he's holding his cellular up to my ear."

"God is so good to provide friends in our time of need!"

Eventually, Paul explained to Jimmy and Lucy the full story of what happened to their son. At the advice of friends, the ailing Paul had gone to the hospital. For two hours he waited in a room full of contagious people before being called in for blood work. His temperature was taken and found to be over 104 degrees; he was told to leave and come back in two hours.

Nearly two hours later, Paul and his friend Mustafa walked along a sidewalk near the Buenos Aires hospital. Mustafa hailed a cab and they rushed back to the hospital, where Paul was placed in a bed. At midnight he was told he would need an appendectomy. The next few hours were a nightmare. If a patient came into the hospital in what appeared to be a worse condition than he, Paul was asked to get out of his bed and give it to the new patient. Waiting meant sitting on the filthy floor. Throughout the night he was moved from bed to bed.

At some point, Paul left his bed to go to the bathroom. Struck by such a terrific pain, he fainted. At this point (it is believed) his appendix ruptured. Over the next ten hours, Paul lay unattended as infection spread throughout his abdomen. Finally, he was wheeled into surgery. "When they gave me the anesthesia and told me to count backward, I fell asleep wondering if it would still be raining when I woke up," Paul explained to his parents. "The surgery took over two hours. When I woke up, I had been wheeled out onto a sidewalk. Sure enough, I awoke in the pouring rain. I thought I had been left there to die! I looked up and saw trees with a lot of birds huddled in the rain. I called for someone to help me, so they would know I wasn't dead. Eventually, someone pushed me back into the ward. As the day wore on, I asked for water, but no one would give me any. Finally, I was moved to a private room and that's when Marcelo came in and prayed with me."

The next few days after her son's surgery, Lucy was heavyhearted and grieving that she couldn't help. Still, in an effort to stay within the bounds of normalcy, she tried to do her housework. As she listened to a tape of James Wilson, she took a moment to pause and concentrate on the words of "His Eye is On the Sparrow." During the song, the Lord clearly spoke to her.

"Lucy," the Lord comforted, *"My eye is on Paul. I am in control."* With that, Lucy released her son into the hands of her heavenly Father.

On September 26, a denominational women's convention in Colorado announced that the son of Jimmy and Lucy McGuire needed prayer. Marcelo's mother had traveled from Argentina to attend the convention, and she joined with hundreds of other women to pray.

The following day, Lucy and Jimmy received a call from a man whom they had never met. "Hi," he said. "My name is Randall Baxter; I'm from Texas. I heard that your son is in pain and away from home. Is that right?"

Jimmy gripped the phone and answered cautiously. "Yes, yes, that's right."

"Well, sir, if you'd like, I can arrange to have American Airlines tickets delivered to him, if you'd like to fly him home."

Jimmy straightened his shoulder. "We certainly would!"

A phone call to Paul revealed that, yes, he could physically make the trip, in spite of the fact that he had spent five days postop without food or water. The tickets were delivered and Paul was taken to an airport, then placed on an American Airlines plane. In Dallas, Randall Baxter's pregnant wife drove to the airport to make certain he was okay as he changed planes. Later, Randall called the McGuires to give them a report.

"I want you to know that your son has made the connection."

"How is he?" Lucy asked.

"My wife says he's in a wheelchair, he looks tired, but he is fine. He said to tell you that he can't wait to get some of his mother's cooking!"

Lucy laughed in relief.

"I'm at work right now," Randall continued, "and I'm tracking his flight on my computer. Paul has flown 3,200 miles and has 3,000 more to go!"

Lucy took a quick breath. *His eye is on the sparrow!*

Jimmy and Lucy met their son at the airport a few hours later. Indeed, he had lost a lot of weight. "Mama," he told her one evening, "I wasn't given any food for five days. The day I was released from the hospital, the nurse brought me some food, but no utensils. I said to her, 'I need utensils to eat.' The nurse turned to me and angrily shouted, 'Do you think this is the United States? You have to bring your own supplies here!'"

Lucy shook her head sadly, wondering how her son would have survived without God's grace and mercy.

Ten days after his return home, Paul had gained eleven pounds. Other than a large, vertical scar, he has recovered perfectly, but with a new perspective on life. "What really surprised me was how God took care of me. I try to enjoy each moment in life for what it brings," he says.

Years have passed, and while Jimmy and Lucy can't say that every conflict or hardship in their marriage drew them closer, they agree that the trauma of their son's illness pulled them to a place of unity. The difference in coming together as God designed a husband and wife to do versus rolling off blame and what-ifs lies within neither of them having anything to do with the cause or the cure. What the McGuires have now learned, firsthand, is that it's simply easier to trust God.

Jimmy and Lucy's Precious Verse:

"Look at the birds of the air; they do not sow or reap or store away in barns, and yet your heavenly Father feeds them. Are you not much more valuable than they? Who of you by worrying can add a single hour to his life? And why do you worry about clothes? See how the lilies of the field grow. They do not labor or spin. Yet I tell you that not even Solomon in all his splendor was dressed like one of these. If

that is how God clothes the grass of the field, which is here today and tomorrow is thrown into the fire, will he not much more clothe you, O you of little faith? So do not worry, saying, 'What shall we eat?' or 'What shall we drink?' or 'What shall we wear?' For the pagans run after all these things, and your heavenly Father knows that you need them. But seek first his kingdom and his righteousness, and all these things will be given to you as well. Therefore do not worry about tomorrow, for tomorrow will worry about itself. Each day has enough trouble of its own."

MATTHEW 6:26–34

A good marriage is that in which each appoints the other guardian of his solitude.

RAINER MARIA RILKE

*Be strong and courageous.
Do not be afraid or terrified because of them,
for the LORD your God goes with you;
he will never leave you nor forsake you."*

DEUTERONOMY 31:6

One True Vow

row old along with me!
The best is yet to be...

ROBERT BROWNING

We begin each day with a prayer and by reading the Word of God. Each night before we go to bed, I turn to Audrey and say, "Good night, Dear. I love you more tonight than I did this morning." Then in the morning when we awake, I turn to her and say, "Good morning, Dear. I love you more this morning than I did last night."

DR. MICHAEL A. GUIDO, Evangelist[†]

I married a Christian. He was my father in the Lord as well as my husband; he led me to the Lord. When we married, I joined his work in evangelism. We traveled constantly! We were married twenty-one years before we ever slept in our own home. Before then, we stayed in people's homes and motels. Michael teased when he said he loved me because I was armed with Lysol. Sometimes it was difficult, but I wouldn't change a thing.

AUDREY F. GUIDO,[†]
Married November 25, 1943

My parents have been married for fifty-five years. After two major strokes, Mother (Sue) has been ill for some time and has been an invalid at home for the last four years. My father (Lewis) is her caregiver by choice. He says, "I have nothing else to do but take care of your momma." Chores include cooking, the laundry, cleaning (including her "accidents"), and shadowing her as she walks with her walker. All that he has done has been in a loving manner. Dad and I hired a bath aide to take care of her three times a week.

Before Mom became ill, I worked full-time, but have since left to work part-time from my home. This enables me to assist them more. However, at one point she stopped eating and drinking. She became ill and was hospitalized for a week. We knew that she was too weak to go home. For the first time, Dad acknowledged that he was tired and didn't know if he could take her back home. The doctor recommended a nursing home for short-term rehab. However, after only a couple of weeks, it was apparent she would need to stay.

Dad wants her home and she wants to go home, but her thought processing is only clear approximately 35 percent of the time. Other times she zones out or is very childlike. I am there daily assisting with her care, and I take Dad out every other day. He didn't realize how tired he really was until he had a chance to rest. He is over eighty years of age.

I truly believe the Lord will be calling Mom home before long. In the interim we are faced with trying to decide her place of residence and care. We ask the Lord for wisdom and discernment regarding what to do and that His will be done no matter what. Perhaps through this brief separation, Dad will be better able to cope with leaving her there and visiting often, or with her death. Death, of course, is the ultimate separation for them in this world. . .but not for eternity. Either way, we are looking at much sorrow in the near future and ask that God will strengthen each and every one of us, to enable us to cope with whatever comes our way and remind us of His promises!

CONNIE KEITH BARRY

Lewis and Sue's Precious Verse:

Let us then approach the throne of grace with confidence, so that we may receive mercy and find grace to help us in our time of need. HEBREWS 4:16

If I could reach up and hold a star
for every time you've made me smile,
the entire evening sky would be in the palm of my hand.

UNKNOWN

I don't remember us ever having any bad words with each other. Then again, Wilbur was a Georgia State Patrolman and he wasn't home a lot. That might have had something to do with it. Wilbur went into the service for two years during World War II. During that time, my mother came to stay with me. I wouldn't have even thought to leave. . .even while he was gone. . .but back then it wasn't as easy as it is today. I wouldn't have even known where to start.

MARY MATTHEWS,
Married December 24, 1939;
separated temporarily by death, December 5, 1994

This [my wife] is it for me.
If I only had Tracey, it'd be enough."

MICHAEL J. FOX,
after being asked how he felt
due to Parkinson's Disease

∞

Let Alone a Lifetime

Hank and Bobbi McGill

Bobbi smiled at her reflection in the mirror. Today was her wedding day, the day she would finally become Mrs. Hank McGill, and she was happy. For the first time in her life, she was happy.

Before 1965, when she met Hank, Bobbi couldn't say with any honesty that she had ever smiled. By the time she was seventeen years old, she had lost both parents to death. Her sister moved far away from their home. This, combined with her history of two failed marriages and six children, gave her little reason to smile. Then she met Hank, who was much younger, but so mature for his age.

"He's so moral, so thoughtful, so caring. . .something I've never experienced before," she now spoke to her reflection. "And," she added brightly, "he's unbelievably good to my children!"

It was two years since their first meeting. In that period of time, Bobbi had seen through Hank that life does indeed hold happiness and was not all losses. Hank's love for Bobbi had been strong from nearly the first day they met, but it took her awhile to let down her guard and allow herself to fall in love.

She had already lost enough.

"But," she reminded her reflection as she spoke to it again, "today is warm and sunny and I'm going to marry Hank."

There was a ten-year difference in their ages; Bobbi was thirty-two and Hank was twenty-two. No one gave them six months, let alone a lifetime. But they knew differently. So did God.

Several months after their wedding, Bobbi awoke one morning to a full-blown migraine. Her moaning alerted Hank, and he turned to her in concern.

"What's wrong?"

"I've got another headache," Bobbi answered, closing her eyes against the blinding pain made more severe by the filtered light in their bedroom.

"Another one?"

"Yeah," Bobbi whispered. "This is the first one since we married, though." Bobbi attempted to get up but was unable to raise her head from the pillow. It didn't take long before the newlyweds knew there was a problem and a doctor needed to be seen.

Over the next several weeks and months, Hank escorted Bobbi to several ENTs (ear, nose, and throat physicians), only to leave angry. No one could give them a straight answer as to the cause of Bobbi's headaches and dizzy spells; a few of them had been downright cruel. One doctor, after shooting cold water into Bobbi's ear (which landed her on the floor), calmly stepped over her supine form, leaving her and Hank alone with the nurse. Later, when he came out of his office, he spoke firmly to Hank. "You need to get her to Mayo Clinic as soon as possible."

Hank and Bobbi cried all the way home. They knew there wasn't enough money in their bank account for such a trip. Moreover, Bobbi and Hank feared Bobbi would die. But God knew otherwise.

Shortly after this, Bobbi spent a month in the hospital because the dizziness had become exacerbated. There she was seen by another ENT who gave her a diagnosis of "a form of Ménière's disease." She was sent home with medication that worked for awhile, but eventually it stopped helping.

This was more than thirty years ago. Eventually, a diagnosis of Ménière's disease, a disorder of the inner ear in which there is no cure, was given. Doctors don't know what causes this disease, though there are many theories.

A person with Ménière's disease lives on a time bomb. Dizzy spells can, and do, strike without warning, leaving the patient on the floor, clutching the carpet as the room spins out of control. When the spell is over, the patient is exhausted and oftentimes will spend hours or days in bed, unable to move or think clearly. For some couples, a disease of such proportion would have ended such a tender marriage. But for Hank and Bobbi, the extraordinary happened.

During the first year of their marriage, Bobbi began to feel the "nudge of God."

"I feel we are supposed to go to church, Hank," Bobbi said one evening as they lay in bed. Bobbi was recuperating from another bout of vertigo.

"I feel that same way, too," Hank said in agreement.

"Gladys has been coming by, giving me Scriptures to read and praying for me," Bobbi said, telling Hank of the older woman's visits.

"Then we'll go to church when you feel you can get out and about."

It was the best decision they ever made. They were soon baptized and have followed the Lord ever since, in spite of the fact that there has been no miracle cure or healing for Bobbi. What there has been, however, is a sweet Presence in their union, a glue holding them together "in sickness, and in health."

"Without God," Bobbi said to Hank one day as he tended to her needs, "you could not have held up under this tremendous load. It's humanly impossible for one man to accomplish in one day what you accomplish."

Hank nodded. "God is good. We don't always understand why, but we continue to trust."

Time has pushed forward. The children have grown to adulthood, and over the years Hank's and Bobbi's lives changed drastically as she became less and less able to do normal wifely duties. Then, in 1994, while they were on vacation in Florida, Bobbi had a severe attack. Fortunately, they were traveling by motor home, and Bobbi was able to lie down for the twelve-hour drive home.

For the next three years, Bobbi was forced to stay in bed. She has "lost" most of what happened during those years, but Hank has remembered it all.

"You never complain, Hank," Bobbi said from her place on their bed. "You are such a blessing to me! You've bathed me; you've even shaved my legs! You work all day, go to the grocery store, cook our meals, wash our clothes, cut the grass, wash the cars, and tend to the garden."

Hank lay next to his wife and reached for her hand. "Without God in our lives, we could never have survived this long." Hank squeezed Bobbi's hand. "Let's sing praises to our Lord now."

Bobbi doesn't remember exactly when the tradition began, but somewhere way back, they began to lie in bed at night, holding hands, singing, and then praying together.

In the past few years, Bobbi has been able to do a little more each month. She is out of bed, doing simple chores such as folding clothes, dusting, or emptying the dishwasher.

"I am so proud of you, Bobbi!" Hank exclaims when he comes home and sees what she has accomplished.

"It's only by God's grace," Bobbi replies.

Hank and Bobbi have celebrated over thirty years of marriage. "Truly," Bobbi said to her husband, "you were sent to me by God. I don't know why you've put up with so much."

"When I took our vows, I meant them. In sickness and in health."

Bobbi smiled knowingly at her husband as she gave him a gentle kiss. "Only God, my love. Only God."

Hank and Bobbi's Precious Verse:

I can do all things through Christ who strengthens me.

PHILIPPIANS 4:13 NKJV

There is a courtesy of the heart;
it is allied to love.
From it springs the purest courtesy
in the outward behavior.

JOHANN WOLFGANG VON GOETHE

With God's Help[†]

Van and Judy Gale

As was her custom, Judy Gale rose early the morning of August 17, 1999, leaving her husband, Van, asleep in the bed. Quietly slipping through the house, she made her way to the computer, switched it on, and waited patiently for the few moments it took to go on-line. For several minutes, she answered E-mail from friends and family. It was a wonderfully peaceful morning, until a strange sound from the master bedroom startled her.

"Good morning," she called out. "You okay?" She waited a moment. When Van didn't answer, she called out again. "Good morning! You okay?"

Several moments ticked by. Judy held her breath, until she heard the sound of her husband's voice. "I'm okay."

But something in his voice sounded strained. Judy's heart stirred and she got up and peeked around the corner into their bedroom. There was Van, lying on the floor next to their bed. The left side of his body appeared totally limp, and he was grasping the bedcovers, trying to pull himself back into bed. A look of confusion clouded his eyes, and Judy immediately recognized they were not focusing. Instinct told her that her husband of but nine years had suffered a stroke; she immediately sat on the floor beside him and cradled him in her arms.

"Father God," she prayed. "I come to You, in Jesus' name, and thank You for Your saving grace. Thank You that Your presence fills this room and wraps around us now. Thank You, Jesus, that by Your Word we have Your promises. It says in Your Word that if two of us agree concerning anything we ask, it will be done for us by You. We are those two. Thank You, Lord, for being our rock and high tower; we run into Your name and are safe. Thank You, Lord, that Your peace goes beyond our understanding and goes ahead of us and is ready for us ahead of time when we need it. We cover ourselves in Your peace. Thank You, Lord, that You are the glory and lifter of Van's head and there will be no further attacks on him. We speak life and health and healing to your body. Be healed. Be well. Be strong. You will live and not die. You will run and not be faint or weary. We release the anointing of God that supplies everything in your body, Van. The same Spirit that raised Christ from the dead dwells in your body, Van, and will quicken you and bring life to your body. We thank You, Lord, for what You are doing here and we give You all the praise, all the honor, and all the glory. We worship You with all our hearts. Thank You for being our all in all."

Judy and Van stayed on the floor for some time, allowing Judy to assess what had happened and to determine, with God's help, what they were to do next. Soon 9-1-1 and Van's physician were called. The ambulance arrived soon thereafter and Van was placed on a gurney and slid through the opened back doors. The paramedics hopped in beside him, and as soon as the doors were closed safely behind them, Van was off to the hospital and Judy was following behind in their car.

Three days later, with his condition listed as stable, Van was transferred to DuPage Convalescent Center, a highly rated facility with a subacute wing for stroke victims.

"I'm not a stroke victim," Van said adamantly. "I'm a stroke victor! We're off to a new adventure of trusting the Lord," he added with a squeeze to Judy's hand.

"Yes, we are!" she agreed.

During the first few days, Van's comments were consistent. "Everything is going to be fine. God is in charge. We have a faithful Father." Judy's heart was confident and full of faith because Van was full of faith. As God had ordained in the beginning of time, Judy was drawing from her husband's love and devotion to the Lord.

With Judy close by, Van was put through an extremely thorough evaluation as to the condition of his extremities, eyesight, and strength. They soon knew that the strength on his left side had been "compromised" as a result of the stroke. As was Van's way, he gave a spiritual outlook to his physical condition. "Don't say 'stroke,' say 'struck!' The devil has struck me on the side of my head!" When they were more certain of the extent of injury to his eyesight, Van commented, "The left half of each of my eyes is on vacation!"

In spite of Van's comical behavior, this was a shock to Judy. Van had always been a reader and could nearly always be found studying, especially the Word of God. Now they were faced with studying something that had been foreign to them previously; they had to learn an entirely new vocabulary of medical and clinical terminology. Their faith, however, stayed constant. "We can do all things through Christ who strengthens us," they quoted frequently. "We are overcomers in the Lord."

When Van began the rigors of physical therapy, the Scripture he and Judy adopted came from Hebrews 12:12–13.

> *Therefore, strengthen your feeble arms and weak knees.*
> *"Make level paths for your feet,"*
> *so that the lame may not be disabled,*
> *but rather healed.*

Judy and Van began to share the Scripture with the various

therapists who tended Van over the next few months. During this time, he learned how to sit, stand, and to walk again. Limbs had to be retrained—all of this a slow process, made easier by their faith in God and the promise from Hebrews. Van spent seventy-three days in rehabilitation. The majority of the effort fell upon him, but Judy's love and support were never far away.

On October 30, 1999, Van returned home, still unable to climb even one stair. Judy had a ramp built for him. On January 3, 2000, he returned to church for the first time since August. The moment was an emotional one for their congregation. Van was the senior pastor and just the day before an associate pastor at the church had lost his battle with cancer and had gone to be with the Lord.

In February, Van began outpatient therapy at a rehabilitation clinic in a nearby town. His days were filled with six one-hour sessions where he learned to read, climb stairs, ride a bike, and do mathematical problems. With God's hand, and Judy's unfailing faith and love, all that Van had lost was being retrained and restored.

"Do you know what I think got us through this difficult time?" Judy asked Van one evening. Without waiting for a reply, she answered, "The Word of God we've kept hidden in our hearts. It does not move over during difficult times. It stays the same and can be counted on. It's our circumstances that change and not God's Word. His Word is solid and can be trusted in all circumstances and situations. He's the *God of the circumstance*."

Life for Van and Judy Gale had changed dramatically in just a few short months. Even the "landscape" of their home changed. They have support bars and handles in the bathrooms, a wheelchair parking sign for their car, more medicine bottles on the dresser, and a wheelchair. One day when Judy was particularly tired and physically aching, she had to come to grips with something she had never before thought about facing. She had just tucked Van in for a nap and returned to the kitchen to finish their lunch dishes. And there they were, tire tracks from the wheelchair had drawn lines in the carpet as though a small car had driven through the living room. Though the sight was only for Judy's eyes, she was overwhelmed. *These should be footprints and not tire tracks!* she thought. A small yelp escaped her lips.

Suddenly, she could no longer catch her breath. She sat down at the kitchen table with her hand cupped over her mouth to catch the sobs. "What is wrong with me, Lord?" she prayed. "I've been through so much in years past and always kept a balance of faith! Why am I suddenly so grieved and sad?"

Judy sat quietly for awhile and waited for the Lord to answer her aching heart. Then, in His intimate way, He said, *It's okay; soon it will be footprints.* A joy came over Judy as she realized God was promising a miracle. Not only for her, but also for her precious husband. She clearly understood that his health was now compromised and she was to be his helper, nurse, coach, encourager, joy-bringer, as well as his therapist. She had promised to honor him when they had married nine years earlier. She had promised to respect and defer to him and be a blessing to him. When they married, she had given him her vow to love and honor him. She had made a covenant with God Himself to come alongside Van as his helper.

As Judy continued to allow the Holy Spirit to minister to her heart, she was filled with such joy and peace. Later, as she read her Scriptures, she found a word of encouragement in Matthew 25:40. "The King will reply, 'I tell you the truth, whatever you did for one of the least of these brothers of mine, you did for me.'"

Judy was doing more than just caring for her loving husband;

she was taking care of Jesus, covered by the body of Van. When she looked upon Van, she could see Jesus on the inside. "How could this be a burden?" she asked her heavenly Father. "Only if I allow it to burden my heart, and I do not. I choose to be true to my vow of love."

This doesn't mean that sometimes the days or nights are not difficult. But when Judy cries out, the Lord always quietly reminds her that Van would do the same for her if the situation were reversed.

Today Van is walking with the help of a cane. "Stutter stepping," he and Judy call it with a chuckle. And they thank God for many things, including the laughter. And, they always count their blessings backward. They count what they do have rather than what they do not have.

"Thank God we can laugh!" Van said to Judy.

"Serve the Lord and never be bored," Judy returned.

They do; they never are.

Van and Judy's Precious Verse:

Consider it pure joy, my brothers, whenever you face trials of many kinds, because you know that the testing of your faith develops perseverance. Perseverance must finish its work so that you may be mature and complete, not lacking anything. JAMES 1:2–4

*Love is swift, sincere, pious, pleasant, gentle,
strong, patient, faithful, prudent, long-suffering,
manly and never seeking her own:
for wheresoever a man seeketh his own,
there he falleth from love.*

THOMAS A KEMPIS
The Imitation of Christ

Resting in His Love

Joel and Lisa Copen

Twenty-four-year-old Lisa Safley answered the ringing telephone on her desk at work. "Hello?"

"Lisa, this is Dr. Winey. The results of your blood work have come back and we have a diagnosis."

Lisa took a deep breath. For the past several months she had bounced from one doctor to the next, searching for a logical diagnosis for the symptoms she had been experiencing. Pain had begun in her wrist, eventually spreading throughout her body. One doctor said it was due to tendonitis. Another said it was due to hammertoes. None of those answers made sense, so after researching on her own, she had finally come to see one last doctor.

"The tests came back positive. You have rheumatoid arthritis."

"Oh. . .I do. . . . Okay. So, what now? Will it improve?"

There was an audible sigh from the other end of the phone. "That's hard to say," she answered. "It's chronic."

Lisa took a moment to assimilate what she had been told. "If normal is a ten, what's the best I can ever hope for?"

With hesitation the doctor answered, "If you're lucky, a five."

"As scary as the words were to hear," Lisa later told her boyfriend Joel, "at least I know what I'm fighting. I can't handle not knowing why I'm in such pain, but I can handle the thought that my life will now be—on a scale of one to ten—a five. Not knowing is the worst. Now I just have to learn to make the most of 'five.'"

What Lisa didn't know, however, was that life would eventually fall down to a "two." Nor was she prepared for the reactions she received from friends and family.

"You're really lucky to have this at such a young age because there's a lot of research going on right now," her landlord, a divorced woman from her church, said soothingly. *Bless her heart,* Lisa thought. *This wasn't the best way she could have given me encouragement, but she's trying!*

Others at church were not as sympathetic. "If you pray harder, God will take it away," some said. Still others remarked, "What have you done wrong to make God mad?" Lisa's mother wanted her to try herbs. . .magnets. . .anything!

"Mom, I've tried enough of the home remedies. Maybe there's a possibility that God might want me to just live with this and see what He can do through it and me?"

"I'm only trying to help, Lisa," her mother responded. "I just hate to see you hurt. I want to be able to fix it like when you were little."

Lisa sighed deeply. "I know, Mom. What mother wouldn't want the best for her child? You're truly wonderful and I love you. Thanks for trying to understand."

Lisa turned back to Joel for comfort. Previously, when Lisa told him the diagnosis, he had responded in the same shock she had felt earlier, but he didn't patronize. "We'll get through this together," he soothed. Lisa slipped her aching body into his tender embrace, resting her head against his strong shoulder. Neither of them realized the long-term impact the diagnosis would have on their lives. In spite of the obvious obstacles, however, in October 1995, Joel asked Lisa to be his wife.

"Are you sure about this?" Lisa asked Joel.

With a roll of his eyes, Joel exclaimed, "Yes!"

"You'll face a lot of obstacles you wouldn't face if you married someone else."

"I know."

"Marriage is hard enough without adding RA to it."

Joel rolled his eyes again. "I know!"

Lisa laughed at the dramatics. "Then the answer is yes!"

Six months later, they married.

"I take comfort in knowing that you knew the real me. . .the one before the illness," Lisa commented to her husband one evening.

"What do you mean?"

"Well, you knew me before RA, and my personality is really still the same; it just gets a bit trapped in this bod."

Joel nodded.

Still, some days, weeks, and even months are difficult. In their first year of marriage, Lisa was in a lot of pain. She began a drug study in which she was placed on a placebo (an innocuous substance used in controlled experiments), resulting in a major physical crash. During that time period, rather than throwing a pity party, Lisa read everything she could get her hands on about writing, including writing for the magazine market. Months later, with a bonus Joel received from work, they purchased a computer. A new world opened up for Lisa.

Soon after, with Joel's support, Lisa began a small group at their church for people with chronic illness. This led to the publishing of a newsletter that eventually went to a national level.

"This is getting too big," Lisa said to Joel one evening. "I've got people wanting to meet each other, wanting pen pals, more chat time, more articles! I'm going to file for nonprofit status. This way people will be able to get tax deductions from their donations, and that's the only way we can make it financially. It will also give us the credibility that we need."

Joel and Lisa spent hours at the local bookstore poring through manuals on how to start a nonprofit organization. They researched fund-raising, marketing, publishing a newsletter, and anything else that might aid them in their new adventure. They often left with a few books to take home and highlight. Eventually Lisa commented, "We can do this ourselves. We don't need to hire an attorney to file the 501(c)(3) status for us. It's just going to take some time." Thus many hours were spent drinking coffee and writing business plans and marketing concepts to reach out to the chronically ill with the message of finding hope in Christ.

Lisa spoke with Joni Eareckson Tada and Tim Hansel about the dream she and Joel had of beginning a national ministry for people in chronic pain. "Go for it!" they both said. "There's nothing out there like this and it's so needed!"

Lisa and Joel did just that. They went for it. Rest Ministries, Inc., was born.

In spite of the victories from God, Joel and Lisa still struggled to meet the needs of her illness and were forced to face certain facts. Joel stood by Lisa through surgeries, the necessity of stronger drugs such as oral chemotherapy, and drug testing that led to extreme dizziness and the constant desire to vomit. At one point, due to the illness, her jaw locked for five days. Each and every day her body battles a constant war against urinary tract infections, staph infections, gynecological problems, ingrown toenails, and the inability to walk farther than across the room. Still, the bond between Joel and Lisa remains strong, and his dedication to her is obvious.

In 1998, Lisa and Joel decided that they were ready to start a family.

"If you want to have a child, you should do it now," Lisa's rheumatologist told her. "I hate to sound negative, but your health isn't going to improve."

Lisa went off all of her medications except prednisone, the only medication that could control the arthritis and that the doctor said would be safe during a pregnancy if it was monitored closely. After twelve months of enduring extreme pain, on low dosages of medication, Joel and Lisa were told that prednisone had stopped ovulation. Lisa was referred to a fertility specialist who put her on six months of medications that helped her begin ovulation. This drug, however, caused other problems that made pregnancy impossible without taking it to the next level, in vitro fertilization.

After discussing alternatives with the fertility specialists and their pastor, Lisa and Joel decided that they would seek adoption, an alternative they had always considered. They went to adoption seminars and found an agency they liked. They began the paperwork and requirements of the application and then started to look for a home.

"Lisa, I think we're ready to buy a house," Joel said.

"It'll have to be one that has only one floor. I couldn't manage stairs on a regular basis," Lisa remarked. In the San Diego area, finding a one-story house, in a safe neighborhood that they could afford, was quite a project. At times, Lisa felt saddened by the search. Joel became her strength, comforting her with his endearing love. Finally a home was found and purchased. By this time, Lisa had also been diagnosed with fibromyalgia.

As Lisa's condition continues to degenerate, her marriage to Joel continues to strengthen; Rest Ministries, Inc. (http://www.restministries.org), continues to reach thousands; and Joel and Lisa continue to wait for a precious bundle of joy to call their own. Until then, they are where God desires them to be, and they feel blessed.

Joel and Lisa's Precious Verse:

My comfort in my suffering is this: Your promise preserves my life.   PSALM 119:50

Two souls with but a single thought,
Two hearts that beat as one.

FRIEDRICH HALM

Anthony and I met and married in Honolulu, Hawaii. We came from extremely different backgrounds. I was an only child of English, Irish, and German descent, born and raised in California. Growing up, I had no religious instruction. My husband was a Catholic Italian, raised in East Boston with a sister and two brothers. His mother had a nice Italian girl picked out for him to marry when he returned home. When he married me, it was a shock to the entire family. We have had many moves and ups and downs during our years of marriage. My husband is a man who has to control everything, which was most upsetting to me, and at times I wanted a separation. We stayed together, though, and we both believe it was because of our marriage vows and commitment to each other. Our parents remained married to each other throughout their lives, and it was a fine example for us. We were blessed with three children, and all three have told us how glad they are that we are together, as so many of their friends' parents divorced. The most important factor is that my husband and I accepted Jesus into our hearts. The Lord be praised.

JEANNE GREGORY,
Married July 31, 1949

Randy was a runner and is still an avid bike rider. He felt tingly in his arms, and sharp spasms like an electrical shock occasionally went down his spine. His sister had been diagnosed with multiple sclerosis fifteen years previously, so we headed immediately for the doctor, who sent us to a gentle, kind neurologist. The possibilities brought about so many feelings and emotions. When we got the diagnosis, we just looked at each other. Randy didn't go back to work that day and neither did I. Instead, we went to a dark, quiet restaurant, ordered a lovely meal, and did not eat. Conversation was in the stunned mode, but we both knew what the other was thinking. We had two children, his mom living with us, five acres, a huge house with a pool that needs constant maintenance, and church activities. Not to mention the athletic lifestyle Randy's maintained since he was a teenager. We couldn't believe that he would get MS!

After leaving the restaurant, we left word for our family that we were going to a movie. We went to see *Hook* and cried all the way through it. Randy related to Peter Pan—loss of the present as we know it, loss of future dreams, and the fear of the unknown being worse than the reality.

That very evening we were paid a visit by the fire chief (Randy's boss) and the head of the board of directors. The purpose of their visit was to offer Randy the position of fire chief. . . effective almost immediately. I'd gone into our bedroom while the men were talking. Randy came in, white as a ghost, and said, "You're not gonna believe this, but. . ." He said he'd tell them tomorrow. They must've thought he was wacko not to jump at the chance! Life is so funny, so odd and surprising! The next morning, he told them "yes!" Sometimes you just take life by the horns and leave the results to God. He'd not failed us yet!

Randy had to deal with all the typical symptoms, but the worst by far were the night terrors. Massive nightmares of demons, chasing, falling. . .awful stuff. . .plagued him. Sweating, tears, screaming out. His arms would jerk up in spasms. We bought a new bed, sheets, down comforter, a leather recliner, even an expensive pillow. We cried. We prayed. He took medication for awhile, but what finally ended it was when I asked my ladies' Bible study bunch to pray. Until then we hadn't shared these horrors with anyone. . .it was just too scary! How silly of us!

The big quirk came when I started having medical problems of my own. Here I thought I was the safe one, and then I was diagnosed with asthma, diabetes, and ulcerative colitis/proctitis. I am on the "Three P" medical plan: pills, potions, and lots of prayer! Randy's able to tell when my blood sugar is too low almost before I know—or when we are walking and my breathing becomes weird and danger might strike. It is so good to depend on him to help. We can hardly believe that we both have these things and are secretly embarrassed, as we are so strong and active and certainly don't want to be defined by our diseases. We are strong disciples of the Lord and know He will be in control of each and every one of our situations. . .as He always has. The devastating fear of the unknown future and the uncertainty as to how to "be there" for each other is what was, at times, difficult. How do you be strong when you're falling apart inside, but faith says be strong and you've got to carry on for the other partner?

The answer is simple, really. We have always had an agape kind of love: seeking the highest good for the other. It has sure come in handy!

PATTI IVERSON †

Randy and Patti's Precious Verse:

"Choose for yourselves this day whom you will serve. . . .
But as for me and my household, we will serve the LORD."

JOSHUA 24:15

*F*or those who think marriage is too hard, that they can't handle it, we are here to say, "God is faithful." Those aren't just words for us. God has sustained Mary Beth and me through some deep valleys—as well as taken us to some incredible mountaintops—and He'll continue to do so.

S<small>TEVEN</small> C<small>URTIS</small> C<small>HAPMAN</small>

*T*he consciousness of being loved softens the keenest pang,
even at the moment of parting;
yes, even the eternal farewell is robbed of half its bitterness
when uttered in accents that breathe love to the last sigh.

J<small>OSEPH</small> A<small>DDISON</small>

A couple of weeks after we officially began dating, Sonny ran out of medicine and had to find a doctor and a pharmacy. He was still new in town and had not made any arrangements. Since we were becoming pretty serious about each other, he said he wanted me to know about a medical condition he had.

"Bren, I need to tell you something important," he said. "I told you my mother was dead, but I did not tell you what she died from. She had diabetes and complete kidney failure. I also have diabetes, and although my kidneys still function, one of them only has partial function. The doctor said I need only one functioning kidney, but there is always a chance that both kidneys could fail like my mom's did. Right now I need to find a doctor here in Phoenix and get a refill on my insulin."

"Insulin?" I asked. "My dad has diabetes and he takes a pill every day."

"He has the adult diabetes. I have what they call juvenile diabetes because it started in my teens."

"What happened?" I didn't know a lot about the disease.

"I collapsed at home one day. I had been having some trouble with my eyes and bad headaches. I had been feeling light-headed a lot, too. The next thing I knew, I woke in a hospital bed with needles everywhere and my sight almost gone. I've been taking insulin shots ever since. I thought you should know now, in case you want to change your mind about seeing me."

"Why should that change my mind?" I replied. "I can walk out the door and get hit by a truck and be dead today. Why should I worry about what might happen in the future? Tomorrow is not promised to anyone, so we'd better concentrate on today."

The second year of our marriage, I discovered I was pregnant. I had wanted a child very badly, even dreaming of holding the child, but it was not to be. Sonny was working nights and I was in bed when the pain started. At first, it was a light cramp like a menstrual pain, then pain exploded in my stomach and the blood started flowing. I lay huddled in the bed in shock until the pain ended, and I stumbled into the bathroom to clean myself up. I felt hollow inside and knew my child was gone. Later, the doctor confirmed my fears. I was no longer pregnant. I cried in Sonny's arms the next morning as I told him what had happened.

Five years into our marriage, he collapsed and was rushed to the hospital, where we learned he only had partial function of his one functioning kidney and would have to be on dialysis for the rest of his life unless he became eligible for a transplant.

I was at work when they called me. I rushed to the hospital and was told they were running tests. After keeping him for two days, the doctors determined his kidneys were not functioning enough to clean the toxins out of his system.

We were together when the doctor told us about the condition of his kidneys. I turned my head for a moment to compose myself, because I knew I had to be strong for Sonny. I listened quietly, then asked the doctor about other options to dialysis. He mentioned the transplant but said unless it was from a first-degree relative, he had little chance of it working. With both of his parents being dead and only two sisters, both with families, I knew the chance was slim. He would not ask them to endanger themselves for him.

The next four years he was in and out of the hospital. He was moved to another hospital that specialized in kidney-related conditions, and a graft was placed in his arm to allow the dialysis machine to clean his blood. He was very sick the first few weeks as they tried to adjust the treatment to take enough but not too much out of his blood. He had problems with the graft during the first year. It tore and I had to rush him to the hospital and a new one was inserted in his arm. That was another surgery. As he adjusted to the routine, he kept trying to work, despite my protests. He would push himself too hard and end up back in the hospital.

Then came the week I experienced a sense of dread. One morning before I left for the early shift at work, I said to Sonny, "Be careful." When I arrived at work, I called him and again cautioned him to be careful. The feeling was so strong I felt a weight on my spirit.

Later that day I received a call from Sonny; he was in the hospital following a car accident. My heart skipped. I rushed to the hospital emergency room, where I discovered that they were releasing him. They gave him pills for his pain and told him to go ahead and take his dialysis treatments. I took him to the dialysis center, and shortly after he was hooked up to the machine, he began experiencing pain in his stomach. I had them page his doctor. He was not sure what was going on but sent for a surgical specialist in internal medicine. When he arrived and examined Sonny, he explained that he felt his spleen was ruptured and that it was necessary to run some tests. Sonny passed out on the table and they rushed him to surgery.

I spent the next four hours in the chapel praying with all my heart for God to save him. I found out later that he died on the table but was revived. He had no fear of death after that.

It had been several years since Sonny had seen his children from his first marriage. His son was fifteen and needed a father's influence. His ex-wife agreed to let his son and daughter stay for the summer, but only if Sonny picked them up. She refused to let them fly out from Louisiana.

He had not been feeling well and asked my uncle and his best friend Bo to go with him to help drive. Because of the length of the trip, he had to stop over in Texas and take a dialysis treatment before continuing to Louisiana. They spent the night with a friend, and the next morning he called me to let me know they would be leaving as soon as his dialysis was over. We talked about the children and how much fun we would have during the summer, how we could take them to the Grand Canyon and maybe Disney World.

Before he hung up, his voice changed. He sounded nervous and a little agitated. He said he did not want to take the dialysis and wished he could get in the car and come back home to me. I told him to do just that, that we would get the kids later. Something in his voice made me regret I had not gone with him. His ex-wife had given us little warning, and it was hard for me to get off for a week on such short notice.

After a few seconds, he responded that he was being silly and he had come too far to turn around now. He said he would be okay.

I had to run some papers to the main office of my job and was gone about half an hour. It was only a block away, so I walked. On the way back, as I mentally planned different things for the summer, I was hit with a blinding pain that caused me to stagger and fall against the wall. I stayed in this position for a few minutes before I was able to get my bearings and continue back to my office. When I arrived, I sat down with my head in my hands, trying to figure out what had happened. I was filled with a deep dread. When the phone rang, it startled me.

The caller identified herself as Gwen, a nurse from the clinic in Texas and a friend we had known for many years from Sonny's dialysis in Phoenix. She was calling to inform me Sonny had died. According to her, right after they put him on the dialysis machine, he complained that he could not breathe. They disconnected him, but he went into cardiac arrest. They rushed him to the hospital, but he was dead on arrival.

When you are hurt, you say cruel things, and what I said to Gwen was cruel. I told her, "I trusted you to take care of him. How could you let him die?" The words hung in the air as I hung up on her weeping voice. I was not proud of what I said, but at the time, my pain blinded me to anyone else's feelings.

I moved through the next few days in a fog, surrounded by family and friends. I managed to make all the funeral arrangements and had his body flown home. At the service, I pulled the wedding ring off my finger and placed it on his finger, then gently kissed him good-bye, taking a final look as they closed his casket for the last time. We had nine years of marriage. Too short, yet filled with more love than some people find in a lifetime. I never regretted my decision to marry him, and despite the hardships of his illness, I loved him more than I ever thought possible.

If I had it to do over again, knowing how many sleepless nights I spent standing vigil in the hospital at his bedside, I would do it again. I know tomorrow is not promised to anyone, and true love accepts no barriers.

BRENDALYN STRICKLIN †

Love is the flower of life,
and blossoms unexpectedly and without law,
and must be plucked where it is found,
and enjoyed for the brief hour of its duration.

D. H. LAWRENCE

Back in those days, growing up in the primitive Baptist Church, you just didn't hear of anyone getting a divorce. I mean, nobody. That didn't mean we didn't have hard times; we did. But when we dedicated our lives to the Lord, we used our faith and trust in Him. I've always been a believer in taking each day as it comes, and that's just the way we did it. One day at a time, trusting in the Lord.

MARY BETH BRANNAN,
Married September 7, 1935;
temporarily separated by death, November 26, 1997

Nothing worth having comes without some kind of a fight.
Got to kick at the darkness 'til it bleeds daylight.

BRUCE COCKBURN

Divorce was not ever an option. When I took my vows, I meant what I said. Above all, I kept my faith in God, and at the end of his life, Ivey had long since stopped drinking and eyeing skirts. We survived the Great Depression together, lost two homes and everything in them to fire, and buried three of our seven children (two during separate Thanksgiving holidays). That's a hurt you never get over. At the end of sixty-six years, it was I who was beside him when he died. In the end, he asked God to forgive him for his sins, and I know one day we'll be together forever. Up there it won't be like it was down here. Up there I'll never shed another tear.

ELMA D. PURVIS, Grandmother of EVA MARIE EVERSON.
Married December 25, 1920;
separated temporarily by death, July 21, 1986;
reunited by God, January 26, 2000

*There is no more lovely,
friendly or charming relationship communion or company,
than a good marriage.*

MARTIN LUTHER

*Marriage has less beauty or safety than the single life.
It's full of sorrow and full of joys.
It lies under more burdens but
is supported by all the strengths of love. . .
. . .and those burdens are delightful.*

UNKNOWN

Hope, Help, and Encouragement for Christian Marriages[2]

Move your priorities around and watch chaos begin, guaranteed! If you desire a solid marriage, build it on *God's foundation;* constantly study God's wisdom on Christian marriage, the roles of husband and wife, and strengthening your walk with the Lord. This results in a firm foundation for your marriage and life. Keep God first in your life always!

This means remaining faithful to God and His Word. This means diligently seeking to understand and obey the Scriptures in one's life. Do you wonder how this works? By walking in constant obedience to God, you will have less opportunity to make the "wrong decisions" and "reap" unpleasant side effects in your life. Following Christ does not mean that you never face trials, but rather when trials come into your life, you will be equipped to understand and handle them.

Following Christ is not easy, though! It is much more than saying you're a Christian. Your life must be an example of the Christian life. If you ever wonder if what you "want" to do is the "Christian" way, ask yourself this question: Could I see Jesus doing this or acting in this manner?

Tips for a Christian Marriage

Keep God FIRST!

Pray together!

Respect and honor each other!

Encourage each other to grow together!

Read the Bible together as much as possible!

Be swift to hear and slow to speak!

Make time to communicate with each other!

Protect and honor your marriage vows!

Do not let others come between you!

Have a "Mission Statement" for your marriage and family!

Thank God every day for your mate and the life you
have together!

Understand that "love" is a choice, not a feeling!
(You must choose every day to love your mate.)

Tips for Tough Times

Pray; ask God for help. Read the Bible, devotionals, and meditate.

Be still.

Let "bad moods" pass. (These are not times to make or tackle big decisions.)

Try not to speak in anger. Cool off first. Words hurt!

Take one day at a time!

Be good to yourself! Know Jesus loves you!

If you don't know what to do, do nothing!

Always be willing to forgive! Some of the most important words in our English language: I'm sorry.

If you are having relationship problems with your mate, ask yourself. . .Am I *choosing* to love this person? Or am I *choosing* not to love?

Do you need to put the "eyes of Jesus" on? What do you see?

Say "I love you!"

*Reach back in your heart
to all those "sweet memories"
you have with your mate!
It's fun to bring them back,
then realize just why you picked this person
to spend your lifetime with!*

Notes

[1] Moore, Geoff. Geoff Moore and the Distance Greatest Hits compact disk. Forefront Records, 1996.
[2] Christian Marriage and Family Website, ©1997–2000 CMF Ministry, http://www.geocities.com/Heartland/Plains/8218/index.html

About the Author

EVA MARIE EVERSON is an author, teacher, and speaker on a variety of subjects designed to develop intimate relationships with God. She writes for several ministries and publications, teaches Old Testament theology at Life Training Center in Orlando, Florida, and is a contributing author for many books. Eva and her husband live in Orlando, and have four children and three grandchildren.

Eva Marie enjoys hearing from her readers and invites you to e-mail her. The address is: BridegroomsBride@aol.com.

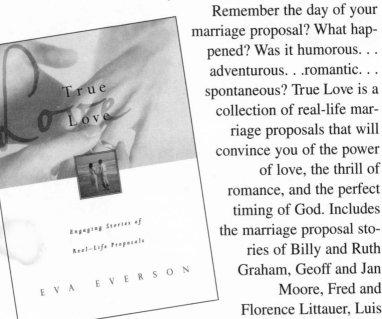